C000184138

AN ILLUSTI
ARCHITECTURA

ALMOST A DECADE has passed ..... the publication of "Dundee – An Illustrated Introduction". Published to coincide with the Centenary of the Dundee Institute of Architects, this popular book superbly illustrated the historical development of the City of Dundee in its beautiful location on the sloping north bank of the River Tay.

I welcome the publication of this fully revised and extended edition. Retitled "Dundee: An Illustrated Architectural Guide", this new book underlines the reality that, essential for the production of good architecture, are clients of vision and civic consciousness. The outstanding quality and variety of architecture revealed in the buildings illustrated emerge as a testament to such clients, the skill of their architects and the respect the city has for its heritage.

This lovely book will be essential reading for all with an interest in cities and architecture and an indispensible guide to the city of Dundee and its hinterland.

J. Fulton

J FULTON
PRESIDENT
Dundee Institute of Architects

© *Authors: Charles McKean, David Walker*
Series consultant: David Walker
Series editor: Charles McKean
Editorial consultant: Duncan McAra
Cover design: Dorothy Steedman, Almond Design
Index: Oula Jones

Royal Incorporation of Architects in Scotland
ISBN 1 873190 09 3
1st published 1984
Reprinted 1993

Cover illustrations
Front: Main Dundee and the Tay from Dudhope (Wishart)
Inset From a series of Saltire Award-winning ceramic panels by Keith Donnelly, in Bellfield Street (Wishart)
Back: Left Ranger Centre, Templeton Woods (Wishart)
Middle Clydesdale Bank, High Street (Wishart)
Right GA Data Processing Centre (Wishart)

Typesetting and picture scans by Almond Design, Edinburgh
Printed by
Pillans & Wilson Ltd, Edinburgh, Glasgow, London and Manchester

Top *Dundee High Street in the 1830s, drawn by Joseph Swan.* Above *Strathmartine Lodging (demolished) after Lamb's* Dundee

INTRODUCTION

If architecture reflects the soul of the city, the soul of Dundee should be revealed by this Guide. But it has been the very devil to categorise. What you notice, first, are the differences from the other great cities of Scotland. Dundee has none of the formal planning so proudly displayed in Edinburgh, Glasgow or Aberdeen; and it has obliterated the ancient topographical features that shaped it – the shoreline and harbour, the Corbie Hill, the Castle Rock, and the Scouring Burn. As a consequence, the impression it now presents to the casual visitor is one of randomness if not incoherence. Yet random and incoherent it is not.

Few cities are universally blessed. Situated on one of the most picturesque firths in Scotland, with its own temperate microclimate, Dundee lay in the path of war, principally during the 16th and 17th centuries. Moreover, Scots cities, pre-ponderantly of stone, were given their character by that stone; and stone proved Dundee's joker – none of Edinburgh's Craigleith or Aberdeen's granite, but something soft, brown pudding-like stone, friable and easily eroded. The thrifty attitude of using stone from the quarried Corbie Hill (now North Lindsay Street) was but a short-term economy. Even then, a strong controlling hand might yet have made something wonderful from Dundee's given advantages – but there's the rub.

Entrepreneurial in spirit from at least the 15th century, international in trade and in outlook, Dundee's prosperity derived from weaving or cloth – and weavers are notoriously independent folk. Persistently radical in religion and politics, the burgh favoured a sturdy individualism rather than the corporate spirit so evident in Edinburgh or Glasgow. Dundee's history was formed by powerful individuals who simply *ganged their ain gait*. The great jute dynasties of the 19th century – the Coxs, Baxters, Grimonds and Gilroys – were only larger in degree, rather than different in kind, from their Dundonian entrepreneurial predecessors.

The sacking of the burgh in 1651 in the Civil War caused a ferocious interruption to the burgh's steadily consolidating prosperity, and grievous hurt. Yet in under 20 years, the town had repaired and rebuilt itself, attaining a prosperity confirmed in substantial mansions and a new Town's Hospital. To judge by the imposing civic buildings added through the 18th century, the town's wealth was ever rising, recognised in the appointment of a Town's Architect, Samuel Bell.

As the tight old burgh became more dense, however, suburbs and villas sprouted east and west. Even Provost Alexander Riddoch, who controlled it virtually single-handedly for 40 years, detached himself from the centre. He commissioned Samuel Bell to build him a pleasant villa on the site of the Town's Hospital out beyond Nethergate.

The sun-kissed eastern approaches – the Cowgate Fields and Forebank – initially proved sufficiently attractive to tempt the Nine Trades to build their new Kirk there in the late 18th century; but by the next century, the Scouring Burn, swiftly pursued by the Dens Burn, attracted threadworks, tanneries, ropeworks and ultimately mills and factories, like wasps to a jam jar. The quality went elsewhere, leaving St Andrew's Church hemmed by industry and tenements.

Nor was the city wholly dependent upon linen or jute, although dominated by them. During the 19th century, it became a centre for whaling, newspapers (a notable dialogue ensuing between the *Courier* and the *Advertiser* before they settled down, married, and became the mighty publishing house of D C Thomson & Co) and jam. James Keiller & Sons represented the only Dundonian industry associated with local produce (the Carse of Gowrie had long been associated with soft fruit), but its reputation lay also with sweets and marmalade. Of these, only journalism thrives.

The principal ambition of Victorian mill owners – and even their engineers, such as Peter Carmichael – became that of ending up as landed gentry with substantial county properties so that one large suburban mansion, with another up to 30 miles away, became the norm. Those of similar ambition but less wealth settled first in the sunny slopes to the east; but were soon overwhelmed as tenements surged out from *c.*1870. Dundee became deprived, as a Victorian Town Clerk lamented, of the energy and acumen of its men of substance playing an appropriate role in the city's affairs. Once those with money or power had quit the centre, it was abandoned to market forces. Overwhelmed by poor people from the

Dundee's domed skyline from City Square with Belmont Hall in the distance

Cox's Stack, Camperdown

Wishart

countryside or (in large numbers) from Ireland looking for work, and riddled with disease, it became desperately vulnerable to clearance for municipal improvement.

Concentrations of 19th-century poverty can be tracked by following Catholic churches which, offering comfort in the worst districts, was predominantly the church of the underdog. Sensing a challenge, Dundee became host to an unusually strong Episcopalian Mission to the poor, led by Bishop Alexander Penrose Forbes, which produced Mission churches of external modesty but internal gorgeousness in West Port and Hilltown; and one of the finest Episcopal cathedrals in Scotland on the Castle Hill itself.

We can only imagine how scandalous conditions must have been to drive the normally *laissez-faire* Dundonians into such civic intervention, so much was it against their nature. And, delayed by 22 years of municipal bankruptcy, they were certainly not prompt off the mark. But when Dundee did decide to act, the result was far-reaching. The 1871 City Improvement Act was deployed as the means not only of constructing new routes through ancient Dundee, but of obliterating relics of the old burgh altogether. Old was out. The vision of Commercial and Whitehall Streets was one of long glittering façades of commercial palaces, similar to those in cities such as Milan and Paris. Relics of pre-1800 Dundee are scant and principally subterranean.

The first Scottish city to plan a Garden Suburb, in Craigie, and the first to construct a housing estate, Dundee moved from total opposition to wholesale support for civic intervention within the space of decades. It provided itself with a new Civic Centre, and excised any corner of old Dundee that constricted traffic.

But by this time, the city's economy was in free-fall. The city's jute decline had proved even more abrupt than its inflation. It had swollen in three successive phases – the 1830s, 1850s and 1870s – and had largely collapsed in 1914, largely because processing and marketing skills had been learnt by the producers of the raw material.

The task facing 20th-century Dundee has been how to create a city of permanence and prosperity from a city with a small, nearly obliterated core, swathed by hastily erected and unplanned shanty towns. It's instinctive attitude after the Second World War was to view its Victorian history as that of an industrial Babylon to be obliterated as a scar on the face of humanity. A new Dundee was to be created, of bypasses, shopping centres and prominent (indeed, very prominent) housing estates. Down came the Overgate, the Wellgate, and the Hilltown, and the city centre was severed from its hinterland by the inner bypass. During the following 35 years Dundee tholed the debilitating experience of extensive dereliction and clearance.

The remarkable change in spirit since 1984 is attributable to a new sense of civic identity founded upon extensive research into Dundee's earlier history. Dundee, like Glasgow, had suffered from the mythology that it had been little more than a couthy and otherwise insignificant market town prior to the arrival of exploitative Victorian capitalist entrepreneurs. It is now evident, however, that pre-jute Dundee was a substantial burgh of notable entrepreneurs upon whose success those linen and jute barons built. In the city's history of industry and mechanical invention, a new generation has found much to be proud of; particularly as those inherited skills have been so adaptable to the new world of microchips.

Such a shift in attitude would naturally be reflected in architecture. Huge stone coffins derelict 10 years ago – such as Tay Works, Seafield and Camperdown – have been transformed utterly into intriguing and popular flats – one indeed into a consumer park. Gaps have been filled, interiors rediscovered, and a new cosmopolitanism abounds in the streets. In short, Dundee's sense of self has been retrieved.

Yet, what is that self? Still difficult to characterise, still largely anti-corporate and still only too frequently favouring the short-term over the best, as on the Shore. It is rather like *Dr Who*: each generation seems utterly different, but remains, at heart, remarkably constant. Given the finest seafront in Scotland, its temperate weather, strong character and engaging history, the question is what will Dundee transform itself into next.

Organisation of this Guide

Text Arrangement
Entries give the name, address, date and architect (if known). Generally, dates given are those of the design of the building (if known). Text in the small column illustrates the history or character of Dundee.

Map References
References in the index refer to page numbers; numbers on maps to numbers against building entries in the text. Maps are intended to be used as a guideline only.

Access
Although many of the buildings described are public and easily accessible, many are private. Users are asked to respect that privacy.

Sponsors
The support of Scottish Enterprise Tayside, the City of Dundee District Council, Tayside Regional Council, Servite, Hillcrest and Cleghorn Housing Associations, and the Landmark Trust, is gratefully acknowledged.

13 Panmure Street

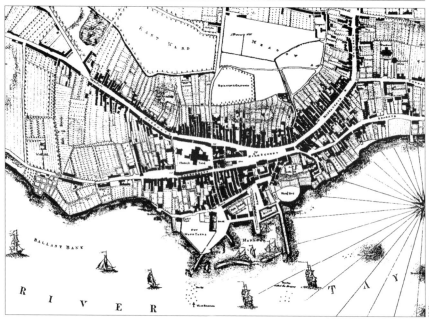

Dundee in the late 18th century

UNDERSTANDING OLD DUNDEE

The language spoken by the inhabitants has, from time immemorial, been broad Scotch; that is English or Saxon with a peculiar provincial accent. That accent evolved into the Dundonian dialect in the 19th century as mill girls had to make themselves audible above the clatter of machinery.

Dundee sits as guard where the Firth of Tay narrows, and controls seaborne entry into the heart of Scotland. Strategically vital, it suffered from more sieges and sackings than almost any other Scots town save Edinburgh. Its castle, which sat upon the Black Rock, was damaged by William Wallace, repaired by Edward I, and obliterated by Robert the Bruce, eventually to be replaced by a statue. From the Middle Ages, the burgh owed its great prosperity to commerce with northern Europe and with the Baltic, to the extent that its merchants in the 16th century maintained

Dundee, c.1592, drawn by Timothy Pont. Seagate and Murraygate are clearly visible. The Old Steeple obscures the centre of the town: Nethergate is barely begun

representatives in most Baltic ports. A Wedderburn of Blackness was resident in Elsinore simply to oversee the family's own customs clearance. For Dundee was closer to the North Countries than Edinburgh by almost two days' sail, and the safety of its *road*, sheltered between St Nicholas Crag and Broughty Point was attractive to mariners.

Perhaps as a consequence of trading ties with those countries, the burgh was at the forefront of religious reform. In 1535, 25 years before the Reformation, 8 burgesses (including a Wedderburn) were forfeited for heresy. Its nurture of other Wedderburns (the authors of the *Gude and Godlie Ballatis* and of plays which *nipp'd cruelly the Papists*) and of the martyr George Wishart, earned it Robert Edward's title *a second Geneva* – and a sore participation in the religious wars of the mid-16th century (for Broughty Castle proved such an excellent disembarkation point for armies).

Overlooked from the north, and with no natural defence from either east or west, Dundee was not a naturally fortified site. Since internal strife had been rare in Scotland, the town's expansion in the 15th century had largely ignored the requirements for fortification, adopting instead an attitude to war of lying low and letting it pass by. Foreigners were astounded. Mary of Guise' French troops were astonished at the town's lack of castle or walls, and the burgesses' reliance instead upon their tightly packed stone houses.

By the end of the 16th century, that was no longer adequate. A city wall was erected from

Dundee's claim to be a second Geneva at the forefront of reform was underpinned by James Wedderburn. Sometime before 1540, he *composed, in the form of tragedie, the beheading of Johne the Baptist, which was acted at the West Port of Dundie, wherein he carped roughlie the abusses and corruptiouns of the Papists. He compiled the Historie of Dionysius ... wherein he likewise nipped the Papists ... This James had a good gift of poesie and made diverse comedeis and tragedeis in the Scottish tongue.* In 1567, with his brothers, John and Robert, Wedderburn penned the *Gude and Godlie Ballatis (ane compendium book of Godly and Spirituall songs collected out of sundrie parts of scripture, with sundrie of other Ballates changed out of prophaine songis for avoyding of sinne and harlotrie).*

So remarkable *were the people of this place for their adherence to true religion, that at the Reformation, it was honoured with the appellation of a second Geneva ... When Scotland was shaking off the yoke of Popery and Idolatry, the people of Dundee were foremost in zeal and activity, and also first in point of time to undertake the pulling down of this superstition.*
Robert Edward, Minister of Murroes, 1678.

Dundee from the sea c.1790. The Town's Hospital lies to the left, the Old Steeple to the centre, the Town House spire centre right, with St Andrew's spire just beyond the Castle Hill

The merciless assault by General Monk took place on 1 Sept. 1651. *The loss of people in the carnage at the storming of the town, appears, on many accounts, to have been great and cannot be estimated at much less than a sixth-part of the whole inhabitants. Of 159 children, born within the 8 months immediately following, no less than 25 are posthumous ... in the 6 succeeding years, the marriages are more numerous than before the siege. But amongst these, 66 are the marriages of English soldiers.*
Robert Small, First Statistical Account, 1793.

Give me leave wrote the verbose English Captain Richard Franck in 1656, *to call it deplorable Dundee; and not to be exprest without a deluge of tears; because storm'd and spoil'd by the rash precipitancy of mercenaries whose rapinous hands put a fatal period to her stately embellishments ... Ah, poor Dundee! torn up by the roots; and thy natives and inhabitants pick't out at the portholes. Blush, O heavens, what an age is this! There was wealth enough to answer their ambitions, and probably that, as soon as anything, betrayed her.*

Houses in Fish Street in the 19th century, after Lamb's 'Dundee'. Note how the stair rises high above the later roof level

McKean

the Shore up to the Nethergate, continuing up the Long Wynd to Overgate (approximately the route of Marketgait) curving round the back of Corbie Hill (now quarried into Lindsay Street) cutting east by where the south wall of the Howff now is, taking a dip at the Scouring Burn, to run north-west along the edge of the Meadows behind Murraygate. The wall then cut east with a gate at the Ladywell, and then down Cowgate (approximately at St Roque's Lane) to Seagate. The ranks of tall stone houses, with access only through narrow closes, would indeed have presented a formidable obstacle to armies approaching the High Street from the north. But the town remained open east and west. What walls existed were demolished by the Marquess of Montrose after his siege in September 1644; although they were built up again immediately thereafter.

With the possible exception of Drogheda, no town suffered so much in the Civil War. On 1 September 1651, General Monk's troops overwhelmed it and put it to the sack. One-sixth of the town's populace was massacred; defenders who negotiated surrender from St Mary's Tower were executed. The plunder, possibly because other Scots towns had despatched their goods to Dundee for safekeeping, was enormous – *the best that was gotted in the Wars throughout the three nations* according to Dr Gumble, General Monk's biographer. As justification for such bloodthirstiness, Gumble accused the town's defenders of *being well drenched in their cups*, an accusation supported by Sir James Balfour's opinion that *the town's men were most of them drunken, lyke so many beasts*. A week's sack and attendant massacre was an unusually savage penalty for drunkenness.

Mythology has it that Dundee suffered near terminal collapse after its sack by Monk, from which it did not emerge until the end of the 18th century. The architecture gives the lie. Until their removal in the late 19th century, many of Dundee's buildings retained unusual traces of the sack by Monk, in that stair-towers and the gables sometimes extended one or two storeys above the buildings to which they were attached. Certainly by approximately 1670, the town had recovered its vigour, but it seems clear that the upper storeys of the great merchants' houses of the earlier period, presumably burnt out in the sack, were cut down and new shallower

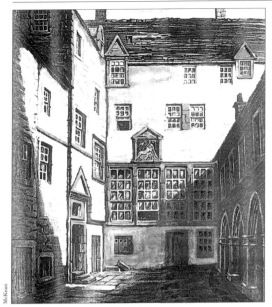

The people of Dundee have been for a long time entitled to the reputation for industry, regularity and economy; and notwithstanding the increase of their wealth and numbers, a just claim to this reputation still continues. As their wealth has been almost entirely the result of great attention and industry, it is preserved by the same virtues, and they are still strangers to extravagance and ruinous luxuries ... This economy does by no means exclude a cheerful and frequent social intercourse, or abridge their real comforts and recreations. It does not even banish a liberal hospitality.
Robert Small, First Statistical Account, 1793.

The Franciscan Nunnery (demolished), off the Overgate: in reality a substantial 1621 town house

pitched roofs inserted. At the same time, enormous, small-paned and deep-set windows of the Netherlandish model were added to many such houses, to the extent that some of them appeared almost curtain-walled. The reviving confidence of the town was reflected in its sophisticated *Town Hospital* (1687), in town houses such as the Strathmartine Lodging (*c*.1700), and the finest civic building in Scotland – the Dundee Town House (1731). The burgh's buildings imply steady and constant improvement, adorning a site of commanding beauty, exceptionally well placed to trade with northern Europe (from which it derived some of its architectural impulse).

Dundee from the south before the arrival of the Discovery; the waste of the city's shoreline only too clearly apparent

9

View from ivory tower: a wintry University's prospect over the Nethergate to the firth

Captain John Slezer's two c.1680 drawings of Dundee (*below and opposite*) depict a substantial port and market town, with a considerable number of opulent stone buildings. The Scots historian, Sir Robert Sibbald, who wrote some of the text for the volume, recorded a town *adorned with excellent buildings of all sorts. It hath two churches, a high steeple, a harbour for ships of burthen, and a considerable traffic with strangers, whence the inhabitants are generally rich, and those who fall into decay have a large hospital provided for them.*

Dundee from the north c.1680 by Slezer. The Town's Hospital seen to the right above Dudhope Castle

Continuing prosperity was marked by a Trades Church to the east (1772), a Trades Hall (1776) and the English Chapel (1783) all by the Town's Architect, Samuel Bell. The canny Provost Riddoch came under pressure to address the bottleneck between High Street and Harbour; and his response was typically parsimonious. Riddoch's roads – Crichton Street (1775) and Castle Street (1785) – were narrow and steep, rather than broad and spacious which brought pressure for further ones in the 19th century. Classical urban design glanced upon Dundee with the opening of Nethergate, Tay Street, Union Street, Reform Street and King Street. Suburbs sprouted to north and west, and the hinterland was sprinkled with late-classical villas.

In 1833, the first of three immense surges in textile production filled the valleys of the Scouring Burn (north-west) and Dens Burn (north-east) with mill buildings and associated industry, particularly foundries. The town centre, encircled by a dense ring of industry, was abandoned by all those who had the choice.

The Town's Plan

Dundee's topography was unique amongst Scottish cities: compressed by the Castle (Black) Rock on the seaward side, and the Corbie Hill and an adjacent bluff on the north, its plan was bound to be linear. In 1678, the Revd Robert Edward, Minister of Murroes, engagingly described it by analogy with a human body flat on its back: two arms outstretched west – the Overgate and Nethergate; and legs –

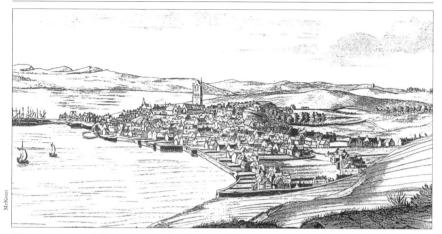

McKean

Murraygate and Seagate – pointing east. Its belly was the market place, its bowels the Shambles (flesh market, properly scoured by the Scouring Burn). The right leg formed the Seagate curving round the Shore, its big toe beckoning to Broughty; the left formed the Murraygate, its foot facing Forfar. This recumbent Dundonian was pinched at the waist, as though by stays – which were only loosened when the Castle Rock was blown up (for Castle Street), the bluff dug out (for Reform Street), and Corbie Hill quarried out (for North Lindsay Street).

Early Dundee on the shore east of Castle Rock was speedily abandoned for the attractions of the more salubrious plateau to the west, around the town's first church, St Clement's, on the site of the City Square. Overtaken in glory, quality and scale by the foundation of the great kirk of St Mary's in the Fields, by the Earl of Huntingdon, it was abandoned and superseded by a tolbooth. St Clement's kirkyard (known as the Vault) was given over to building (in like manner to St Giles' kirkyard in Edinburgh being given over to Parliament Square). So, Dundee was only a seaside burgh at its eastern extremity, where the Seagate houses curved round the edge of the bay, garden walls washed by tides. The harbour, developed from tidal docks west of the Castle Rock approximately at the foot of Crichton Street, was reached, originally, by only two routes: Skirling's (or Tendall's) Wynd which ran south-west behind the Tolbooth; and Spalding's (the Abbot's or Couttie's) Wynd, due south from the Nethergate.

Dundee from the east, drawn by Slezer. Note the town gateway to Seagate, and the Pierson Lodging at the harbour edge

Dundee had depended upon a textile economy to a degree unique in Scotland ever since the Middle Ages. Hector Boece wrote of his home town in the early 16th century: *Dundee, the town quhair we were born, quhair many virtuous and lauborius pepill are in making of cloth.* It was the source of its wealth, raised Dundee to the fourth largest town in the Kingdom, and paid for its fine Renaissance buildings many of which survived to the 19th century. It also encouraged a sturdy individualism, competitiveness and anti-corporate attitude. In the 19th century, however, Dundee's singularity was that it had become so dependent upon the single product of jute; and that the majority of jute workers were females. Well above 60% of the total working population in 1912 were women. Only 23% of the men were over 20, most being boys employed in mills. As late as 1904, one in every four infants died, which the Medical Officer of Health attributed to *the exceptional industrial conditions of Dundee, the very low wages paid to the unskilled male workers in our mills and factories, and the large number of women employed in them.*

Originally, mills were located where water power was available, and of the 30 major industrial survivors in Dundee, 17 lie to the west in the valley of the (culverted) Scouring Burn, and five to the east along the Dens Burn.

At the architectural peak of old Dundee, *c.*1845, the burgh was feeling smug, if municipally bankrupt (in the hands of trustees till 1864). New roads, smashed through the hills and rookeries, had opened out the Market Place: **Reform Street** surged north to the High School, **Castle Street** south down to the docks and the **Exchange Coffee House**, **Crichton Street**, down to the **Greenmarket**, and **Union Street** down to the pier. Renaissance Dundee was not yet so totally abandoned into the slums that it was to become. The High Street remained the centre of Dundee, its Market Place, and the focus for all the trade of a substantial hinterland, draining into here from as far away as the River Dee, Coupar Angus, and possibly Forfar and Montrose. The goods which formerly had to be transferred on to the mules to be sieved down through the closes or down Tendall's Wynd to the harbour, could now travel uninterruptedly and speedily by cart or carriage.

Visiting Old Dundee

Sea-borne visitors to late 18th-century Dundee would have been approaching one of the most pleasant and prosperous towns in Scotland. As they negotiated the Ross Head breakwater, they would have been greeted by a long skyline of domes and spires against the backdrop of Corbie Hill, the Law and the Sidlaws. To the west, the Town's Hospital, then the towering Auld Steeple dominating all, the Town House spire, the Trades Hall dome, St Andrew's spire, and the tall statue atop the Castle Hill.

It was a substantial, busy if quite workaday community. You had to pass by the flesh and fish markets, and several woodyards before making your way up into the centre. But that way was gracious. An enormous balustered sundial on the pier marked the beginning of a tree-lined paved walk which led past Piranesi-

Right The Pierson Lodging, as it may have looked when first built. *Below* Dundee, drawn on a summer's evening from the Ross Head breakwater by Alexander Robertson, *c.*1774

like warehouses up the Greenmarket (the town's reception area), to the East Shore and the back of the town proper. To the left stood **Provost Pierson's** great house (on the waterfront when first built *c.*1600) standing upon arcades, with conical-capped round towers and a tall chimneyed skyline, as though it were on a Baltic shore. Its superstructure, by then, (like so many of the older mansions in Fish Street) had been truncated by and rebuilt after the 1651 sack. Turning right into Tendall's Wynd, you would have had a glimpse of the Vault on the left, the district downhill and seaward of the Town House, with its galleried timber market, and unusually smart **Strathmartine Lodging**: a nobleman's hôtel closing the south side of the Vault (which was once a fashionable location to judge from its arcaded west side). Dutch-inspired, the Lodging had a domed, octagonal entrance staircase and an elegant forecourt. Passing through the narrowing cliffs of the Wynd, you may also have noticed, just before debouching into the High Street, the courtyard of the Laird of **Affleck's** (or Auchinleck's) **Lodging**, with its corbelled stair-tower, large, 17th-century windows, and wayward string-courses and other details of an earlier period.

Dundee's High Street (colour page 49)
The town's market place was similar in breadth to Edinburgh's (*c.*100ft) but less regular in shape. Just before the plateau sloped down eastwards towards the Scouring Burn, the vista was closed by the domed Trades Hall. To the south west, the view was closed by the pedimented English Chapel, whereas a corbelled stair-tower of General Monk's lodging marked the entrance to the Overgate. To the

The Strathmartine Lodging, the Vault (demolished): drawn by MacGibbon & Ross

When Thomas Morer, an army chaplain, visited Dundee in 1666, he was *handsomely treated at the charges of the Corporation.* He though it a *very pretty town at the bottom of a hill ... furnished with two or three small piers for the conveniency of shipping, and the buildings are such as speak the substance and riches of the place.*

Lands of the Greyfriars (now the **Civic Graveyard**) lay beyond the bluff out of sight to the north, and those of the Red Friars, with their hospice for the poor and travellers, along the Tay cliffs to the west, rebuilt in 1678 as *a large and splendid hospital for old men* with a garden running down to the river. U-plan, with corner stair-towers and a central cupola, it was an excellent public building within the Scottish tradition. Vacated in 1746, and used for French prisoners of war and a grammar school, it was eventually replaced by the Catholic Cathedral (see p.66). **Dudhope Castle** (see p.111), seat of the Hereditary Constables of Dundee, lay to the north-west, out of sight, on the slopes of the Law.

The Executive: dedicated by the satirist Henry Harwood to the members of the Guildry: the Nine Incorporate Trades, and Burgesses standing right in front of the Trades Hall. Narrows of the Murraygate to the left, opening into the smart new Castle Street on the right

13

Top right *Dundee High Street c.1900, the Town House on the right.*
Top left *William Adam's original plan from 'Vitruvius Scoticus'.*
Above *Former Council Chambers*

north-east lay the Murraygate leading to the industrial quarter of the Wellgate, with its four large tanneries and three threadworks. In the pleasant Cowgate Garden beyond, basked the Trades' new St Andrew's Kirk. A further smattering of industry, such as ropeworks, threadworks and the like, clustered by the Dens Burn on the far side of the Cowgate Garden. The High Street no longer presented the six-storeyed uniformity of Edinburgh's – and perhaps it never had. Space being more plentiful in Dundee, courtyard houses and palaces were to be found down closes with an abundance impossible in the Capital. The Market Place, with its Cross and its Tron, would have felt like the hub of a substantial country market town, stone walls, colourfully harled, and unbroken from east to west. There were undoubtedly some arcades, but they lacked the regularity of those in Elgin, Glasgow or Edinburgh.

Visitors were also drawn by General Monk's residence in the towered tenement at the Overgate corner, the timber-gabled mansion of Our Lady Warkstairs opposite, and the promise of even more elaborate wanders up the closes.

Mid-way along the south wall of this imposing space, William Adam erected the most elegant **Town House** in Scotland in 1731. The ground-level piazza (known as the Pillars, and focus for all trysting and feeing in Dundee), a sophisticated re-statement of the arcades of the Scottish Renaissance, projected full width into the street (colour page 50). Through this building, Dundee was expressing a vigorous confidence unique in urban Scotland at the time. The principal floor of its seven-bay frontage was lined by tall, baroque windows, each one capped by an oculus. Its central three bays were framed by pairs of

pilasters supporting a pediment with twin oculi above, capped by a steeple. Its glory was the set of rooms on the principal floor, and the fine, oval staircase (the hopelessly insecure gaol in the attic was replaced by others in the cellar). So long as the High Street remained unpenetrated, the Town House took pride of place, until its demolition in 1932.

Forty years later, the Town's Architect, Samuel Bell, used it as the inspiration for further aggrandisement of the High Street. He closed the eastern end with the **Trades Hall** (1776, demolished) whose gable faced west to that of the Union Hall (originally English Chapel, 1783, also demolished). The Trades Hall façade echoed the central, pedimented three-bay section of the Town House, similarly pedimented, Ionic-columned rather than pilastered, two oculi in the pediment framing a coat of arms (saved, along with other relics, in a chamber in St Mary's Tower): the composition dominated by dome and cupola. The **Union Hall**, closing the west vista, was less

Classical Dundee
Above *Trades Hall (demolished).*
Top *Original drawing by Samuel Bell.* Top left *Town House (demolished).* Left *Union Hall (demolished)*

15

The historian, Dr A H Millar, claimed to have converted Caird, a few days before his death, to the retention of the old Town House to enhance the new. The latter died before communicating any such conversion, and the Town House was demolished. Millar subsequently attacked the city to the Historical Association of Scotland: *the despicable philistinism which masquerades under the name of modern utility has lately run riot in Dundee, as in other Scots burghs, and has reached a stage when firm protests must be raised against reckless demolition.*

elaborate: a single oculus in the pediment, one above each window which flanked the principal Venetian window. These design motifs were to continue to be influential in the forward development of Dundee (not least in the **Royal Bank of Scotland**, 1899, on the corner of Castle Street). Those public buildings reflected the substance and wealth of 18th-century Dundee: both lasted barely 100 years, demolished in the 1871 Improvement Act for road widenings by William Mackison, leaving the **Clydesdale Bank**, originally behind the Trades Hall, a diminutive object, inadequate to the task of closing the High Street vista. The formality of the entry to Castle Street being immediately in front of the Trades Hall, was nullified.

As the stone walls of the High Street were punctured by new roads, the space lost its integrity and scale. The Town House was criticised as lacking in dignity. Its crumbling, soft stone had been re-cased in cement which had required frequent repainting. The combination of an inconspicuous site and crumbling façade fostered the view that it was inadequately representative of a great city. James Caird's offer of a new City Hall presumed its demolition, so as to enhance the setting of his munificence; and the grand old building was toppled in 1932.

City Square – presentation drawing of the original scheme for the flanking buildings designed by Frank Thomson for his father prior to Burnet's report. Note the ghost of a dome appearing over the back of the Caird Hall

1 **CITY SQUARE**, 1924–31, Sir John Burnet
Dundee's first piece of formal civic planning upon the oldest civic location in the city, but nothing like as imposing as the 1911 proposal by James Thomson for the **Earl Grey Dock**. The plan proposed two wings of shops flanking the Caird Hall upon its raised platform at the rear, the **City Chambers**, above the western,

RIAS Collection

Proposal for a new City Hall in the docks by James Thomson (unfulfilled)

and offices above the eastern. The design was much modified during erection, 1930–1, by James MacLellan Brown. Burnet's original quality remains apparent in Crichton Street, but City Square's dignity is weak-chinned and sterile. Had MacLellan Brown's cornice been higher, his mansard roof invisible, and his window reveals deeper, the ensemble would have been more distinctive. Relics of the old Town House – griffin banister stops and the cut-glass chandelier – survive in the Council Chamber. Dundee District Council (DDC) Architects have begun the task of making the City Square genuinely civic with planting, lamp-standards, fountains and sculpture.

Caird Hall, 1914–22, James Thomson
Opulently cavernous concert hall in stone-clad steel and concrete, paper-thin plaster panels within executed by Scott Morton. James Caird,

James Thomson, extraordinarily able father of two architects, Harry and Frank, succeeded William Alexander as City Architect in 1904, and William Mackison as City Engineer two years later. His development plan for Dundee was far ahead of its time: a northern bypass (Kingsway), a Garden Suburb for the working class (Craigie), purpose-designed elephantine Civic Centre on the site of Earl Grey Dock (ironic that Tayside Regional Council rents a commercial office block on virtually the same site), and the invention of the road-widening safeguarding line (which destroys townscape by requiring new buildings to be set back). His were the first peripheral housing estates, and – in Logie – the first district heated housing scheme in Britain.

The Caird Hall

The Royal Bank. Above *Original drawing.* Right *As first completed*

Clydesdale Bank. Above *As it is now.* Below *Original drawing for façade*

a jute baron, offered Dundee a new City Hall and Concert Hall just before the First World War; the colonnade was an afterthought, gifted by Caird's sister, Mrs Marryat, allegedly to compensate Dundee for the loss of the *Pillars.* Urban legend places in this hall Sir Thomas Beecham's invitation to Dundonians to throw marmalade at him, should they dislike his performance (provided that they removed it from the jar first). The truth is entirely the opposite. The audience attempted to win an encore by enhanced applause: Sir Thomas responded that encores required prior gifts, and that he expected rows of little pots of marmalade on the platform. (colour page 50)

28 High Street, *c.*1785
Formerly harled four-storey block with quoined angles and wall-head gable, representative of the plainer burgh architecture at the first stirrings of the textile boom.

Royal Bank of Scotland, 3–4 High Street, 1899, Sir George Washington Browne
Money talking: splendid baroque banking palace with giant Ionic arcades, surmounted by an entablature of oculi, parapet and obelisks. High glass-domed banking hall lavishly modernised with costly marble.

2 **Clydesdale Bank**, 94–96 High Street, 1876, William Spence
Triangular pavilion never intended to close the east end of the market place. Its giant Corinthian order appears pygmy in this setting. Despite its richly sculptured Renaissance details, the bank requires another storey or two if it is to fulfil its urban design role.

3 **St Paul's Episcopal Cathedral Church**, Castle Hill, 1853, Sir George Gilbert Scott
One of the finest examples of the high-flown and aristocratic Gothic Revival (appropriate for Episcopalians), clutched to the side of Dundee's ancient castle rock. Built for the Evangelical Bishop Alexander Penrose Forbes, this superb church soars skywards in a way that won it support from the very beginning. It exploits the rise of the Castle Hill to accentuate its great height (210ft) – an unusually impressive urban location for a Victorian church, with the added dignity of being approached up three large flights of steps. Broad, spacious and airy within

St Paul's Cathedral. Below *The steeple.* Below left *Original perspective*

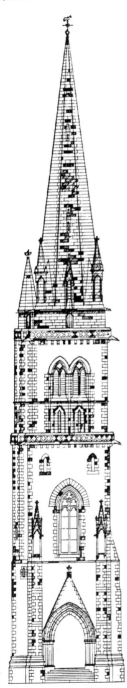

RCAHMS

Simpson & Brown

19

The new Episcopal Church on the Castle Hill seems destined to form a striking instance of the prejudice a fine building may suffer from an ill-chosen site, considered the Building Chronicle in 1854. It is hemmed in on the west by tall buildings, with scarcely a footpath around it, while all around the other sides a glimpse can only be got of its elaborate features through rifts between old houses. The Ecclesiologist (the journal of the Oxford Movement, sole arbiters of architectural propriety in the Gothic Revival) differed. The Church, it said gains much by its unequalled site – a steep rock springing up from the midst of the old quarter of a populous town. The skill of its designer is, however, shown in his having made the most of this opportunity. The treatment is purely Northern and Teutonic, like the plan of the building itself. In it, everything fits into its own place and is in harmony with the remaining structure. The really excellent glass by Mr Hardman which fills all the windows of the apse. is a great additional embellishment. St Paul's stands high among the Churches of the Revival. All concerned in the undertaking have to congratulate themselves on a rare success. In the nave everything is sacrificed to height, and the effect is worth the sacrifice ... we most heartily congratulate Mr Scott on this very successful work.

Gardyne's House as it may have been

as light filters through its many windows: reredos by Scott, mosaics by Salviati of Venice (colour page 49). **Castle Hill House**, 1 High Street, incorporates slight remnants of Dundee's castle. A late 18th-century three-storey merchant's house in provincial classical: dressed stone details and quoins, a bow facing south and a later two-storey porch. Elegance restored by vivid lime rendering by Simpson & Brown. Immediately downhill, incorporated into the 19th-century remodelling of the Castle Mills, is a single-storey arcade which may have screened some form of covered market, for which a grid of pier foundations survive: and another arcade, probably added as a new 17th-century façade to earlier buildings of which lower storeys survive in the basement of Central Bar.

4 **Gardyne's House**, Gray's Close, 70–73 High Street, 1600
Hidden up a close behind the oldest row of buildings (all seemingly 18th century but probably earlier) facing the High Street, this five-storey (much cut down from the original) substantial L-plan merchant's house has a split gable, corbelled oriel, string-courses and echoes of other grandeur. It once contained tempera ceilings. Ambitious proposal for the restoration by the Makaris Guild. There is a timeless feel to its little courtyard at the rear of this row of buildings.

Overgate Centre, 1963, Ian Burke, Hugh Martin & Partners
Commemorates the Overgate (formerly Argylisgait), the principal western route from Dundee, site of a Royal Mint, birthplace of the Scots historian Hector Boece, and – in the towered building on its corner – the birthplace of the Duchess of Monmouth. Post-war Dundee preferred a new shopping centre to the slums of the Overgate, in the days before conservation had been invented.

Reform Street, 1832, George Angus
The first street to follow William Burn's 1824 proposals for the improvement of the town, Reform Street was cut through the bluff to open the High Street to the north. Focused upon the Doric pediment of the High Street (see p.13), it is the finest neoclassical street in Dundee, and the only one to achieve the conjunction of adequate breadth, length and

Left *Bank of Scotland, 34 Reform Street*. Below *Reform Street from City Square*. Bottom *Elevation of the west side by George Angus*

coherence of design comparable to New Town streets then being built in Aberdeen, Edinburgh, Glasgow and Perth. Regency in flavour, each building was designed (rather like Robert Adam's plans for Glasgow) to have shops, uniformly pilastered and balustraded, punctuated by Greek Ionic doorpieces to business chambers and flats above.

Meadow House, Reform Street, 1867, James Maclaren
Headquarters of the Alliance Trust (built as Lamb's Temperance Hotel), it was designed as an architectural riposte to the National Bank across the street. Lamb was a notoriously idiosyncratic citizen whose son collected a vast archive of drawings, sketches and other memorabilia (now in the City Library) many of which he reproduced in his elephantine volume *Dundee: Its Quaint and Historic Buildings*. The project virtually bankrupted his family, but preserved the history of Dundee for posterity.

7–25 Bank Street

In the late 18th century, Dundee had no route to the sea in which two carriages or carts could pass each other. The Council, then under the dictatorial thumb of Provost Alexander Riddoch, anticipated the necessity for new streets – Crichton, Castle and Tay. Prior to the opening of Crichton, Riddoch obtained much of the necessary land: an early example of Tammany Hall politics in the burgh. The new streets, although wider than before, were narrower and more poorly laid out than contemporary developments in Edinburgh and Glasgow.

Specsavers, 16 Reform Street (colour page 50) Breathtakingly impressive interior with very elaborate plasterwork – close-up scrutiny from the mezzanine to the rear. **Royal Bank of Scotland**, 1863, William Scott, is a variation on George Angus's original design – Doric pilasters and a *piano nobile* enriched with consoles and pediments. The **Old Bank Bar**, No 34, 1840, William Burn, ignored Angus's design in favour of an imposing Italian Renaissance palace to act as corner stop. Remodelled and extended *a posteriori*, 1880, by George Shaw Aitken, original features survive within.

5 **7–9 Bank Street**, from 1859, Charles Edward Sumptuous offices for Sir John Leng, the most outstanding editor of the Dundee Advertiser and pioneer of illustrated daily papers. Extended by Charles & Leslie Ower, and awaiting re-use. Bank Street was notorious for the Kinnaird Hall (demolished), through whose high-arched roof a suffragette was lowered to embarrass Winston Churchill during his unsuccessful candidature for Dundee West.

6 **Crichton Street**, from 1779 Dundee's first post-medieval route from the High Street to harbour, created when the Council purchased Dr Crichton's mansion *for a new street to go down to the Shore for the more*

Crichton Street: Below *The smooth east façade*. Right *The west side: note the extraordinary oriel windows of 11–13*

Castle Street: Top left *Looking north to the High Street*. Above *Proposed alterations to the former Theatre Royal*. Below *The stunning façade of No 40*

convenience of the public. It was done too meanly and too narrowly. The east side is now engorged by the polished posterior of Burnet's City Chambers. The west, slightly curving on its slope, is quaint. **11–13** Crichton Street, W J Anderson, is a splendid confection in brilliantly coloured brickwork, oriel windows poking through arches, a flamboyantly curvilinear gable above. The dusky **Royal Insurance Company**, 1971, is by James Parr & Partners.

Castle Street, from 1785
The second street broke out of the High Street immediately in front of the old Trades House, gouged through the castle rock by force of gunpowder. It was more formal and more gracious, but still steep and insufficiently broad. The vista downhill used formerly to be a glorious one of the docks: much of its panache has been forfeited now that the view is down to the Tay Bridge road spaghetti. Most buildings date from the early 19th century.

7 **Theatre Royal**, 7–21 Castle Street, Samuel Bell
The façade (all that remains) retains its dignified pediment with a bust of Shakespeare in its roundel. **26 Castle Chambers**, *c*.1825, a good house (now architect's office), has a rusticated plinth with fanlit door in the centre, polished upper storeys separated by a string-course, architraves above the window, design capped by a cornice. Pleasing plasterwork and columns within.

40 Castle Street, 1919, Frank Thomson
Sumptuous polished granite vestibule to the adjacent office block for the whisky magnate, Sir John Stewart (who committed suicide in 1924). Thomson's first designs were rejected with the instruction that he had to return by

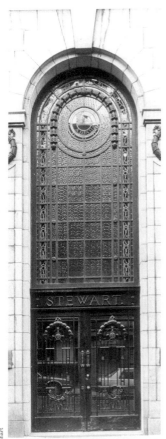

Former Exchange Coffee House: note the lettering – 'City Assembly Rooms'. Once on the very edge of the Earl Grey Dock

Sir John Stewart, *a Lloyd George Whisky Baronet ... a bootlegging pal of Mr Lloyd George* (according to his creditors) had purchased his baronetcy from Maundy Gregory for £50,000 – later refunded by the Lloyd George fund when bankruptcy threatened.

Perspective by George Smith

lunchtime with better if he wished to retain the commission. The lavish interior of this entrance is barrel-vaulted over the staircase, with pictorial glass. The corner block with **Exchange Street**, plainly elegant with Greek Doric columns, was designed in 1832 by David Mackenzie, one of three architect brothers.

At Dundee, the harbour, by great labour and expense, has been rendered a very safe and agreeable station for vessels; and from this circumstance the town has become the chief emporium not only of Angus but of Perthshire. The citizens here (whose houses resemble palaces) are so eminent in regard to their skill in industry and business that they have got more rivals than equals in the Kingdom.
Robert Edward, Minister of Murroes, 1678.

[8] **Winter's** (former Exchange Coffee House), 15 Shore Street, 1828, George Smith
Designed as a coffee house, assembly rooms, merchants' library and reading room, its construction was a public statement of mercantile affluence. Principal rooms were on the first floor, signalled by the elegant Ionic order supported by the more squat Doric base of the ground floor. Original interior, notably the staircase at the centre, and coved ceiling to the main hall.

RCAHMS

THE SHORE, HARBOUR & DOCKS

When Daniel Defoe visited Dundee in 1723, he observed linen trade with England, trade with Norway, Danzig, Königsberg and Riga, and the import of iron, tar, copper, pitch and timber from Sweden. In the 19th century, it was to become jute and whaling. Yet, until then, Dundee remained niggardly in the treatment of its principal income-generator. Its harbours and wharves remained entirely tidal – the Council investing no money despite an increase in trade. The attitude taken to the ferry to Fife was nonchalant: *the ferry was so badly managed, it might have been said to have been no ferry at all – the boatmen being almost constantly the judges of the times of sailing as well as the regulators to the amount of fare ... extortion and incivility produced their certain result – almost a total ruin to the concern.*

Simple mercantile pressures overwhelmed Provost Riddoch and his parsimonious Council. Thomas Telford was appointed to produce a floating dock and graving dock, initiating almost a century of continuous dockland expansion and improvement. By 1912, the harbour occupied 119 acres – entirely land reclaimed from the river – totalling 3.5 miles of

The harbour from the river c.1784.

Thomas Telford was invited to construct *an extensive floating dock and graving dock for large vessels* which Robert Southey (Poet Laureate), who accompanied Telford on one of his nationwide site visits, thought *the finest graving dock I ever saw.* The year after its completion, Dundee had doubled the tonnage levels of 1813. In 1831, Telford proposed 55ft-wide cast-iron lock gates to convert the eastern tidal dock into an enclosed harbour. Supervised by harbour engineer James Leslie, the project was completed three years later and named the Earl Grey Dock.

Harbour improvements in progress, 1836. Note the extent to which Dundee was being removed from its shoreline

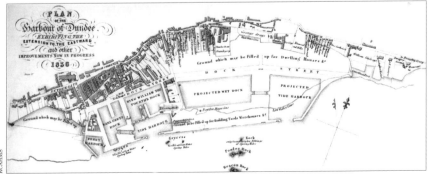

RCAHMS

It is difficult to appreciate just how busy Dundee's port was in the 19th century when coping with jute from India and whalers from the South Atlantic. In 1870, 216 ships and 18 whalers registered at Dundee were trading with the entire known world. Its whaling fleet was immortalised in a sea shanty:

O the noble fleet of whalers out sailing from Dundee
Well manned by British sailors to work them on the sea;
On the western ocean passage none with them can compare,
For there's not a ship could make the trip as the Baleana, I declare

Stanley C Turner

Dundee University Library

Above right *King William IV Dock, c.1890.* Above *The Baleana.* Bottom right *RRS Discovery*

quayside, serviced by 10 miles of railway, handling over 800,000 tonnes of trade annually. Dundee never rose to James Thomson's grand plan for a civic centre on Earl Grey Dock; nor has it ever adequately valued its wonderful south-facing sea frontage. Its shoreline, one of the most magnificent in Europe, has (despite repeated stern warnings by the Dundee Institute of Architects) been developed in a nondescript manner partly impelled by the pressure that *something must be done* rather than ensuring that it is the right thing. Defoe was impressed by the paved, tree-lined walk that once enticed visitors from harbour to High Street: what has happened to that urbane civility today? (Colour page 50)

The Royal Research Ship
Discovery, (right and colour page 51), built by Dundee Shipbuilders for the National Antarctic Expedition 1901–4, was the first ship to be designed and built specifically for scientific research. Dundee had been chosen because of its proven skill in constructing whalers capable of withstanding Atlantic ice. Launched in Dundee in 1901, the *Discovery* had the novelty of a double hull. When Scott of the Antarctic was first trapped in ice in 1904 in the *Discovery*, it was two other Dundee ships – the *Terra Nova* and *Morning* – which rescued him. In 1929, *Discovery* revisited the Antarctic with the British, Australian & New Zealand Antarctic Expedition under Sir Douglas Mawson. After lying neglected for many years, it returned to Dundee in 1986, and has been substantially refurbished. Particularly splendid fittings in the Officers' Ward Room.

8a **Discovery Quay**, 1993,
Michael Laird Partnership
Focal point of Dundee's western quayside. Its brief forbade excessive height, required that all façades should be a front one, and favoured the imagery of a pavilion. In a Botanic Garden, it would not do badly as a Palm House: three-

Wishart

Public warehouse (demolished) – a wonderfully stern design by William Robertson of Leven, 1758

storey, octagonal, domed and largely glazed. Exhibitions and auditorium at ground level, viewing terraces, functional and education areas above. Hard nautical landscape, stone sets, capstans, etc. *Open to the public*

The red-towered **Caledonian Dundee West** railway station has gone: Dundee Tay Bridge station is now in its third incarnation. **Yeaman Shore** has been engulfed by the Inner Ring Road, the principal western landmark being the patterned-brick **Revenue Offices**, the Holmes Partnership, and the more Dundonian **Tay Hotel**, 1898, Robert Hunter – which itself owes much of its personality to William Mackison's Whitehall Crescent (see p.62). The **Olympia Leisure Centre**, 1974, James Parr & Partners, is good if uninspiring of its time: square, enclosed and low lying within motorway spaghetti. It has been enlivened by retrofit by DDC Architects, a ceramic mural and a glazed observation platform to follow.

Tayside House, 1976, James Parr & Partners
One might well question whether the Tay Bridge, or this block, should have penetrated so far into the navel of the burgh. Given that they have, and accepting that a Regional Headquarters is an

In 1873, the Greenmarket was described by W J Smith as *greatly frequented on Saturday evenings, the attractions being of an extremely varied and diverse character. In close juxtaposition may be seen the street preacher addressing the crowd, the quack doctor vending his nostrums, the cheap John and the ballad singer, galvanic batteries, beef and sweetie stands, and exhibitions of dead and living wonders, forming altogether a curious medley.*

Left *Tay Bridge Station concourse.* Below *Tay Hotel (originally Mather's Hotel)*

Thomas Telford criticised the Council's parsimony toward its harbour and wharves, particularly since *the prosperity of the port was connected with that of the district at large ... From the past conduct of the Corporation, and their confined views, no prospect existed of obtaining suitable accommodation under their management, as indeed was fully evidenced by their instructions to me ... A number of public spirited individuals having interposed and overpowered the Corporation, the exclusive management of the harbour was put into the hands of Public Commissioners ... The management of the port was taken out of (their) hands because their views did not keep pace with the growing demands of commerce.*

Top Right *Dock Street, c.1850. Public warehouses on the left, the Coffee House in middle-left distance.* Below *Sailors' Home.* Below right *The arrival of Queen Victoria at King William Dock.* Bottom *Tay Road Bridge*

administrative building (and that site restrictions compelled a narrow one), this tall elegant block of offices does rather well.

Much of the Shore is difficult to reach. **Morton's Bond**, 23–31 Dock Street, 1835, is a late-Regency house absorbed within a much larger warehouse complex. Until a fire, it retained much of its historic interior. Between Gellatly Street and Candle Lane, there is a good assembly of vigour: **57–59 East Dock Street**, 1880, J Murray Robertson, has octagonal bays rising into timbered dormer windows. (Former) Hynd's chandler's shop next door, C & L Ower, is squeezed up into a shapely gable. The **Sailors' Home**, 1881, David Maclaren, was built philanthropically to keep visiting sailors from temptation and robbery. The higher the storey, the classier the apartments with Captain's apartments at the top. Elegant stone Renaissance-detailed block with cast-iron mullions. **Dundee, Perth &**

London Shipping Co (once home for the Falklands Islands Company) was designed, 1891, by James Maclaren.

Dundee Foundry, 40 East Dock Street, 1870 Iron-framed engine works for the Gourlay brothers whose handsome east façade consists of three large doors each capped by an oculus.

Above *Customs House*. Left *Architect's perspective*

9 **Customs House** & **Harbour Chambers**, 1842–3, James Leslie & John Taylor
A symbol of what has been lost, this was one of the largest Customs Houses in Scotland: three-storey, 13 bays long, dominated by a massively projecting centre, capped by a pediment supported by four huge Ionic columns, themselves standing upon an arched, rusticated ground floor. Two separate buildings lie behind the façade, each with fine apartments – particularly the Board Room, and the Dundee Port Authority's Chief Executive's 1930's office suite in the extension. Echoes of a haunted past in the attic loft. Restored by Gauldie Wright & Partners.

The celebrated engineer Ove Arup chose Stannergate for the landfall of his original high-level Tay Bridge so that it could join Kingsway and the regional road network. Dundee preferred a bridge into Dundee, and obliterated its central area and docks to make way for it. Arup's award-winning little footbridge in Durham was of the sort he had in mind for the Tay.

Camperdown Docks, 1857, Charles Ower (Snr)
One must be grateful for any water near central Dundee: and the docks have a nostalgic atmosphere of a Sleeping Beauty wishing to be

Camperdown Dock, old steeple in the centre, clocktower warehouse to the right

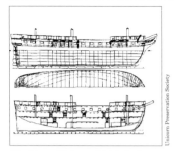

The frigate Unicorn: Right *On its way to restoration.* Above *Section and elevation*

kissed back to life. Roughly rectangular 8.5 acre dock, retaining, on west side, transit shed with cast-iron pilasters with lion rainwater heads. The **Victoria Dock**, begun 1833 by James Leslie to Thomas Telford's design, was completed 1869–75 by David Cunningham, Harbour Engineer; 10.7 acres, rectangular, with swingbridges. The **Clock Tower warehouse**, 1877, David Cunningham, is tall, six-storey Italianate with a clock tower. The dock's finest possession, amidst Naval and North Sea oil vessels, is the frigate *Unicorn*, 1824, a lone survivor of *Britain's wooden walls*. This fine vessel with 46 guns was brought to Dundee in 1873 as a drill ship from the reserve fleet (colour page 51). Being restored gradually by voluntary effort, the splendour of its timberwork is coming to life again. Duck or grouse within.

Harbour Workshops, Marine Parade, 1837, James Leslie
Rare survival of a haulage and repair workshop for the Panmure Shipyard. A steam engine hauled vessels up the ramp for repair. Interior retains the flavour of a Victorian workshop with its smiddy, steam irons, forges and rigging loft.

SEAGATE

When I first came to the town in 1756, wrote a 1799 commentator, *there were very few inhabitants in this street; some old homes near the east end, with several homes in ruins, but chiefly yards ... The only tolerable dwelling homes were Provost Robertson's on the north side ... and some old homes opposite.* The town had inexorably moved west, and as the docks swelled eastwards the Seagate was beached as an industrial backland. It is now a traffic route.

Head of the Seagate in the late 19th century prior to the cutting of Commercial Street

Spanphoto/RIAS Collection

The head of the Seagate as it became. St Paul's Cathedral on the left, and the Seagate Gallery (Robertson's Bond, see over page) on the right

*A **comparison** betwixt what [Dundee] is now and what it was 40 years ago ... Its population has been more than doubled; its charities have risen from £1900 to £7000; its shipping has increased fourfold; and its linen trade been almost entirely called into existence. But the reverse side of the picture must not be concealed. The assessment for the poor has advanced tenfold ... In population, manufactures and trade; in the luxury and comfort which prevail, Dundee has perhaps advanced faster than any similar town in the Kingdom.*
Second Statistical Account, 1833.

Magnum House (former SCWS), 138–140 Seagate, 1934, Cornelius Armour
Turns the corner in stylish American art deco: concrete frame with sleek ashlar cladding surrounding orange-painted metal curtain walling. Unfortunate upper storey added on conversion to flats.

Watson's Bond, 99 Seagate/Candle Lane/Trades Lane, 1907, Johnston & Baxter
Four large five-storey bonded warehouses, reinforced concrete framed and brick clad. Surreal deployment of classical and Scots detail in red brick – tripartite windows, giant four-storey arcades, Diocletian windows, mock-military corbelled and crenellated parapet with an unbelievable crow-stepped gable. The **North Bond**, facing Seagate, is better because sterner: ashlar base, pilasters and pediment. All this fancy stuff conceals the fact that the South, Mid and North Bonds are of reinforced concrete framed and floored on the Hennebique system, with flat concrete roofs.

Loyal Order of Ancient Shepherds, 97 Seagate, 1907, Johnston & Baxter, is a confident Edwardian building in red brick and

Watson's Bond

RCAHMS

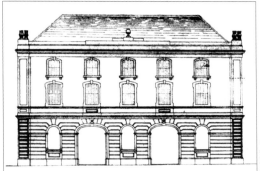

Right *No 2 warehouse*. Above
Seagate Clock

lighter ashlar bands, with vaguely Jacobean
details: blushingly scrubbed and in multiple use.

Seagate No 2 Warehouse, 1868,
Christopher Bissett
Ashlar bonded warehouse for Stewart's Whisky
– plain front facing the street topped by
wheatsheaf chimneys: elegant façade down
Candle Lane. Now flats.

**Seagate Gallery & Printmakers'
Workshop**, Robertson's Bond, 36–40 Seagate,
1897, Johnston & Baxter, is a fairly confident
piece of urban commerce. Less elaborate, but
within the same family, as the exuberance in
Hope Street, Glasgow.

Oh! dear me, the mill's gaen fest,
Puir wee shifters canna get a rest,
Shiftin' bobbins coarse and fine,
Wha wad work for two and nine.

The poor wee shifters were
children, working half time, and
earning half the 5s 6d weekly wage
of the older children working full
time.
Juteopolis: Dr William Walker

10 **St Roque's Library**, Blackscroft, 1910,
James Thomson
Blackscroft lies just outside the eastern
boundary of old Dundee, in the district of
Wallace-Craigie. The Library took the form of a
French pavilion – a kind of *petit Trianon* – in its
formal triangular garden overlooking the Tay.

St Roque's Library

It was laid out as a landscape garden, with a beautiful Italian balustrade and terrace, a sundial, a fountain and trees and flowers – making a new public park in the midst of what had been a very sordid district. The building itself was designed chiefly as a reading room for newspapers and magazines, with a special portion reserved for ladies. It may have been the work of the unfortunately named London draughtsman William Careless. Currently seeking a new purpose.

11 **The Dens Mills**, Princes Street/ St Roque's Lane, 1865–6, Peter Carmichael Dundee has no finer Victorian symbol than the Dens Mills, once the empire of the mighty Baxter brothers who, between 1840–90, rose to be the world's first linen manufacturers. Development began in 1821, and expanded during the three textile booms of 1833–5, 1864–7 and 1871–4. **Lower Dens** was built from Baxter's own foundry. The family had the sense to admit an outsider into their partnership – the engineer Peter Carmichael. It was on his enquiring and innovative genius that the Baxters thrived – and kept the Dens mills on flax, and not on jute. Carmichael's single-mindedness can be inferred from the way he spent his annual holiday: *it was*

The Dens Mills, as became customary, were self contained communities employing their own schoolmasters to educate schoolchildren. At their peak in 1871, the Baxters employed some 5000 workers, 2000 more than Cox in Lochee, one-tenth of all those employed in jute, flax and linen in Scotland. Given conditions of the time, the Baxters did not appear to be unreasonable employers: although anti-union, their paternalistic attitude appeared to ensure reasonable conditions. Mill working created an entire sub-culture of language, behaviour and initiation rites. Strict class distinctions were observed amongst workers, at the top being the weavers: *the weavers, winders and sack machinists are a hard-working, thrifty and self-respecting class of worker. They impress the visitors by their neatness of their dress and the decorum of their manners. There is nothing of the typical mill girl about them ...*
Dundee Social Union: 1912

The Dens Mills: Left *Aerial view of Upper and Lower Dens after redevelopment. Lower Dens at bottom left, new housing top right.* Below *Elevation of the Bell Mill, Lower Dens.* Below left *Cross-section of one of the mill buildings*

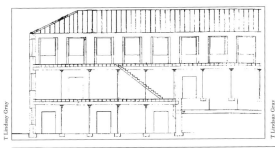

my custom to make an annual excursion in the quest of mechanical improvements. Lower Dens consists of four fireproof flax mills: the **Bell Mill**, 1866, with its superb Italian bellcote modelled upon that of Santa Maria Della Salute in Venice; the **North Mill**, 1935, the **Dens Mill**, 1865, and **St Roque's**, 1830–89.

12 **Upper Dens**, 2 Princes Street, 1833, Umpherston & Kerr (colour page 51)
Once a town in itself. At its peak, Upper Dens comprised a mill, wet spinning mill, calendar press, five-shed power loom factory, three warehouses, two foundries, a further calendar, and two schools. Peter Carmichael inherited an earlier building, and doubled it in size to its present proportions in 1850, with the assistance of Randolph Elliott & Co, adding a Gothic cast-iron attic and a spired bellcote.

The Dens Mills: Top *Cross-section through Upper Dens as rebuilt.* Above *The commanding sight of Lower Dens from above.* Right *The High Mill, Upper Dens, converted to housing with new housing alongside*

Upper Dens was subject to a £7.5m award-winning housing redevelopment and landscaping over 6.5 acres of inner city land. The new-build has been to an appropriate large scale to match the conservation of the existing buildings. The principal Upper Dens mill has been converted into 73 flats for the Hillcrest Housing Association by Baxter Clark & Paul. Excellent landscape and public art, and inspired casting of the engine house as the entrance to the flats.

COWGATE

Historic street overwhelmed by tanneries, breweries and mills, which developed into the market headquarters of the linen industry. It was long the custom of Dundee's merchants to use, as a Rialto, St Andrew's Square – at the head of the Cowgate where King Street now debouches. The late-Georgian bow-fronted gusset with King Street was head office and sometime home of the Grimond jute barons, who desired the addition of the heavy classical embellishments from Edward & Robertson in 1877. The pleasant shallow bay-fronted Georgian houses form the rear of early 19th-century classical homes in **King Street**. It is impossible to tell whether they were added *a posteriori*. **37–39** Cowgate, opposite, an early 18th-century building re-fronted in the Regency period, is in need of care and attention. The restoration of the western end of the Cowgate is a townscape necessity now that the thoroughfare has been severed by the Inner Ring Road (despite the ameliorating quality of its detail and landscaping).

The Cowgate & St Andrew's Square: Below *The Cowgate gusset as altered for the Grimond jute family*. Below left *The same building before alteration, on the right, with its graceful bow facing St Andrew's Square: the meeting place of Dundee merchants before the cutting of King Street. The Cowgate Garden has become a memory*

13 **Wishart Arch**, pre–1548
Relic of the City walls. Although the Arch, main carriage arch and footway arch, would offer only token resistance to armed invasion, it may well have performed more effectively as a mercantile barrier to prevent cut-price goods entering the tightly controlled city. The Reformer, George Wishart, is said to have used the gate as a pulpit from which to preach during the 1544 plague: which legend prevented its demolition. Recently restored by W Murray Jack. The post-modern blocks of coloured flats, 1991, for Gowrie Housing Association, on the site of the Calendar Works, are by the Parr Partnership.

(Former) **Wishart Memorial Church**, 106–116 Cowgate, 1844
Heaven above Hell: U-plan galleried church (with cast-iron Corinthian columns) and anthemion decoration perched above the John o' Groats bar. The missionary Mary Slessor worshipped here 1869–76. Stained glass memorial window in the McManus Galleries.

King Street
One of the most ornamental parts of the town, with substantial, regular and handsome buildings erected on each side, it was opened in the late 18th century to provide an easier route to Forfar and the north-east than the precipitous Hilltown. Unlike Cowgate, it was provided with a good bridge over the Dens Burn. Like a Dundonian Holy Corner, it is ornamented with several fine churches to spice the douce late Georgian

Below *Wishart Memorial Church, 1899*

terraces. The red stone **Wishart Centre**, 1899, T M Cappon, displays the sinuous art nouveau hand of Cappon's assistant W G Lamond in the west façade and wrought-iron railings.

14 **5–19 King Street**, 1815–19, probably David Neave Truncated terrace of marooned classical houses with fanlights, rusticated ground floors and Doric doorpieces – many sadly painted, disfigured or badly maintained. **Glasite Chapel**, 4 King Street, 1777, a simple white-harled octagon with stone dressings and a prismatic slate roof for which no architect is known. Monument to the 18th-century minister, the Revd John Glas, who seceded to form his own sect (they married very young and were given kail (cabbage) soup when attending service – hence the nickname the Kail Kirk). Gutted to become **St Andrew's Church Hall**, its exterior exemplifies fine spare geometry in the Scottish tradition, like the church at Killin (see *Stirling & The Trossachs* in this series).

15 **St Andrew's Church**, 1772, Samuel Bell Imposing rectangular Trades church to a design possibly adapted from one by James Craig, designer of Edinburgh's New Town, and sufficiently impressive to be taken as the model for the one in Banff (see *Banff & Buchan* in this series). Thomas Pennant, who saw the church the year it was completed, thought it *built in a style that does credit to the place, and which shows the enlargement of mind in the Presbyterians*. Built in the semi-rural Cowgate Garden, its construction signalled the growing wealth of the Nine Trades. The fine stone dressings of the exterior are set against rubble (should be harl), with twin Venetian and

Top *The remnant of King Street, possibly Dundee's most gracious neoclassical development.* Middle *Interior of St Mary's Sisterhood Chapel. It was a charming 18th-century house integrating this highly decorated chapel by G E Street at the rear (demolished).* Above *Glasite Chapel*

St Andrew's Church, gracious even without its harling. Above Drawn in 1772, a graceful harled rectangle resting within the Cowgate Garden

The Ladywell, origin of Wellgate and one of the three principal sources of Dundee's water until the mid-19th century, was famous for its purity. In 1868, however, the Water Commission attributed its attractive – piquant – flavour to *nothing but a very purified form of sewage, to the properties of decomposition of which it owes its pleasant flavour ... horribly polluted by sewage and by animal matter of the most disgusting origin. Dundee had remained an unhealthy city long after others had remedied the matter from 1860 onwards,* wrote the Chief Sanitary Inspector; *smallpox, typhus, typhoid and gastric fevers were serious menaces to the health of the community. For many years, there were never less than 300 to 500 cases.*

The north side of Murraygate acted as buffer to the marshlands beyond: *the meadows or greens were then unenclosed, wet and dirty, and the health of the inhabitants was much infected from stagnant pools there. A small narrow close below Quaker Lighton's long tithed land [was] called the Meadow entry; and there was no other entry from the town to the Meadows but it and James Mathew's Close in the Murraygate.*

semicircular arched windows, swags, dominated by its splendid steeple progressively set back at each higher stage in James Gibbs' manner. It retains the splendid civic atmosphere of the Nine Trades, with their banners and chairs and outstanding stained glass. There are, as there were then *seats for the Convenors of the Trades and other dignitaries in the front of the church gallery, and there they sat with their gold chains ... The Minister bowed to them at the close of the service, and they stood up and returned the bow.* (colour page 51)

Wellgate Centre, 1977,
James Parr & Partners
Wellgate formed part of the ancient route from the High Street through Murraygate up Hilltown, to Strathmartine and Forfar. The incline was so severe that the street ended in the Wellgate Steps, an echo of which survives in the northern entrance to the Shopping Centre and Library. This enclosed, three level shopping centre, originally in brown blockwork and protruding brown fascia, was revamped 1992–3 by McColl Scotland with an atrium, a replica of historic streetscape, cast-iron, stained glass and green metalwork. The traders combined with the Council to resurrect a fine old lamp-standard above the steps to Victoria Road.

County Bingo (former King's Theatre),
Frank Thomson
Red sandstone baroque designed by post when Thomson was assistant at Niven & Wigglesworth

in London. His brother provided him with an inaccurate site survey: the consequence only apparent during construction when the pit entrance appeared high above the pavement. Thomson sought help from his father, City Engineer, who obligingly constructed public lavatories under the road at the appropriate point, necessitating raising both road and pavement level to (by coincidence) the requisite height. Well-preserved sections, including marble staircase, basement bar and original domed ceiling, lie dormant beneath later accretions just waiting to be rediscovered.

MURRAYGATE

For a long time Dundee's principal commercial street, it was originally divided into the Narrows (as it bridged over the Scouring Burn) and the Broad, further east. The distinction was eliminated by the 1871 gouging of Commercial Street and the culverting of the river. Here gathered those mid 18th-century landed gentry *who (like the woodcocks) did the honour to pass the winter amongst us, strutted about on tiptoe and in sullen hauteur*. The houses were *of moderate height and, in general, regular and well built*. Once the city failed to prevent its backlands from being overrun by breweries, tanneries and threadworks, the squires quit for the Nethergate, and the Murraygate became the place where *the greater part of business of Dundee with foreign parts is transacted*. In time, that also passed on. Yet Murraygate remains the most engaging single street in the city centre; and its pedestrianisation provides rare relief and some humour in this traffic-dominated city. The landscape, 1992–3, Gillespies, incorporates the tramlines, stone paving and new setts and extensive public art, and specially designed

The Water War, over how to supply fresh water to the city, began in 1832: one faction believing that a rate should be raised to lay on a full supply, the other that it was a commercial operation. How like today! The Nine Trades took a Thatcherite view: they did not see *the peculiar circumstances that should make men idiots enough to prefer paying by taxation what ought to be vendable in the market like any other commodity*. Three separate schemes were proposed between 1833 and 1837, and blocked; £32,000 had been added to the Town's debts with nothing to show for it. *Never was there a dispute conducted with more heart and acerbity as the Water War* according to William Norrie. *Persons who had been the dearest friends for years turned into the most rancorous foes: fathers quarrelled with sons, and brothers with brothers*. It was not until 1874 that the principal water supply from Lintrathen was established.

The Murraygate: Below left Looking north-east to the Wellgate. Below The Old Narrows looking west to the Trades Hall. This was the bridge over the Scouring Burn, a bottleneck demolished for Commercial Street

Dundee Art Galleries & Museums

Wishart

RIAS Collection

The Dundee Public Arts programme evolved from the success of that in Blackness in which a strong working relationship was developed to enrich the environment. The entire city was studied for fifty locations. There is sculpture by Jake Kempsell in Princes Street, standing sculpture in the fountains of the City Square by Lizanne Wood, and architectural embellishments in Upper Dens, including gargoyles by Francis Pelly, etched aluminium panels by John O'Reardon, and brick panels by John Gray.

Above *Potter's Shoe Shop (now Radio Rentals).* Right *Bank of Scotland, original drawing.* Below *Interior*

street furniture by David Wilson. Dragon sculpture by Tony Morrow, and mosaic in front of John Menzies by Elizabeth McFall.
Prime sites always get redeveloped, and the 1980s nearly did for Murraygate. **Radio Rentals**, 14–16, an unsympathetic shopfront, occupies a 1911 Arts & Crafts shoeshop (Potter's) transformed by Gauldie & Hardie from a substantial 18th-century house already on this site. **Meadow Entry**, 16–20, David Rait, 1783, a simple tenement with wall-head gable above an arched pend, recollects the time when this street represented the northern boundary of the town. Rebuilt 1987, Hugh Martin & Partners and Comprehensive Design, in the style of its predecessor, a kink in the street front indicating where architects changed. **30**, 1984, J & F Johnston, is arcaded in brown brick – and **42–4**, 1984, is similarly nondescript. **John Menzies**, 1924, has the brash glazed-fin style (connotations of cinema entertainment) which was the corporate style of Woolworth's (which built it) at the time. **62–68**, 1987, McLaren Murdoch & Hamilton, plugged Pullar's Close – note clock tower and glazed upper floor.

On the south side, **7–11**, 1896, W Alexander, forms part of the rebuilt Narrows – typical of 1871 Improvement Act architecture. **31** has a delaminating classical doorway grafted, in 1887 by Ireland & Maclaren (whose office it was), on to a late Georgian building.

16 **Bank of Scotland**, 29–35 Murraygate, 1858, David Cousin
Classical banker's palazzo – finest in Dundee – built for the British Linen Bank, whose

John Gray

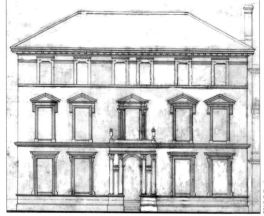

RIAS Collection

The south side of Murraygate: note the original Marks & Spencer

architect Cousin was. This 1854 extract from the *Building Chronicle* indicates that what we see is a graft upon an earlier structure: *The British Linen Bank premises in Murraygate are being enlarged and improved by the erection of a new telling room in the rear, and the extension of the front building ... The front is to be remodelled by the insertion of a string-course, and crowned by a ponderous cornice and balustrade. The new telling room at the rear is very grand with a rotunda supported on Corinthian columns.* **Marks & Spencer**, next door, is one of the few surviving original designs by Robert Lutyens (Sir Edwin's son). **Dorothy Perkin's, 51**, 1984, Hobart & Heron, is plain brown neo-vernacular with window margins above an overscaled shopfront. **53–63**, 1988, Carl Fisher Sibbald, replaced 18th-century four-storey residential buildings by a vigorous similarly scaled block of offices and shops symmetrically disposed around the pend to Peter Street (pedimented and dated above). Similar pediment to Seagate; shallow incised pilasters. **65–69**, 1988, Carl Fisher Sibbald is the extraordinary remodelling of a blank 1960's façade in

At Cooper's Tavern, Murraygate, transpired the comic arrest of two American medical students in 1801. Scunnered by their strange garb and John Bristed's blue spectacles, the landlord refused admittance. They proceeded to harangue him in Latin, which he took to be French. He locked them in an upper room and summoned the Militia. After considerable commotion, during which the Captain of the Militia, Alexander Riddoch, proposed that *on account of the terror and alarm, into which these two ragged tatterdemalions have thrown all the valorous inhabitants of Dundee, somewhat more than twenty-five-thousand people, you could not punish them more effectively than making them militia men in my company.* They were rescued by being identified by a fellow Edinburgh medical student who lived at Magdalen Yard.

Bottom left *53–63 Murraygate with the entrance pend to Peter Street.* Below *Peter Street in the late 19th century looking up to the pend into Murraygate*

birthday-cake architecture with pink buttresses and corbels *meant to be fun contrasting deliberately with its neighbours, introducing fresh colour and focus.* A distinct improvement on its predecessor if only for the way in which the heavily modelled upper storey catches the light. **71–78**, 1991, acts as buttress to Baldragon House, 1910, next door, designed by James Sibbald (architect's great uncle). Polished red brick with artificial stone, tall first floor over glazed shop; columns, aedicules and veranda to roof.

Commercial Street: Below *The east façade sweeping down to the harbour.* Middle *Drawing of the Murraygate corner.* Bottom *The 1900 extension to Commercial Street: note how the scale has risen to six storeys*

Commercial Street, 1871, William Mackison City Improvement Act architecture with the aid of John Lessels: the rhythm of florid Renaissance details has a collective scale and grandeur that reminds one of contemporary Milan – and brings to Dundee a taste of the architectural cohesiveness that its rigidly independent anti-planning stance foiled elsewhere. *The Builder* disagreed in 1898: *only so many yards of patternbook architecture, a mere medley of tawdry ornaments, the sort of thing that might be expected from one of the gentlemen who builds roads and £20 houses in the suburbs. We understand that the Burgh Engineer is responsible for the design ... Everyone capable of judging architectural design must regret that a man who is probably exceptionally capable (he would hardly be Burgh Engineer of Dundee if he were not) should have committed such an error of judgment as to attempt work for which his training and experience obviously have not fitted him.* The stretch between Murraygate and Seagate comprise (with Whitehall Street and Crescent) the largest undertakings following the 1871 City Improvement Act, driven through the heart of the old town *leaving wide streets, open spaces and stately buildings*. It was designed, 1877, by Alexander Johnston: and pressure was applied to ensure that his elevations followed Mackison's designs. Maclaren & Aitken, who designed the French **Calcutta Buildings**, 1877, were more independent, but John Bruce's 1877 **Seagate** corner knuckled under appropriately.

William Mackison, the Burgh Engineer so lambasted by *The Builder*, was certainly capable. Trained as architect and engineer with his uncle Francis Mackison in Stirling, he became its Burgh Surveyor and Town's Architect. With David Bryce, he was the first Fellow of the RIBA in Scotland. When Dundee's engineer, Fulton, quit to go cattle ranching in Texas, Mackison came to the city as engineer, and speedily undermined Scott, the ailing Town's Architect. The Burgh acquiesced, hoping to obtain buckshee architectural services from its engineer. Mackison, however, was cannily putting it on the slate. In 1906, he claimed £40,000 for additional work undertaken outside his normal duties. Suspended and then dismissed, he took Dundee to the High Court but died before the case was heard. His family pursued it to the House of Lords, ruining themselves in the process.

McManus Galleries

7 **McManus Galleries** (former Albert Institute), 1865–7, Sir George Gilbert Scott
Memorials to Prince Albert were the rage throughout Britain, but Dundee was bankrupt. The Baxters, their friends and dynastic rivals formed a private company to build one in time for the arrival of the British Association in 1867, producing the grandest Albert Memorial outside London, *primarily intended as a reference library for students*. Adapting part of an earlier unbuilt scheme for Hamburg's Rathaus, Scott desired to give this project *such national characteristics as to render it distinctly Scottish in general feeling*: which may explain the giant crow-stepped gables and corner turrets. He was proud of the result, writing later of Glasgow University *I adopted a style which I may call my own invention, having already initiated it at the Albert Institute in Dundee. It is simply a 13th- or 14th-century secular style, with the addition of certain*

A new setting for the McManus Galleries? Proposals for possible pedestrianisation

Jute, Jam and Journalism are Dundee's three principal contributions to British culture. Although jute survives yet, only journalism survives in its native habitat with its former vigour. Thomson's is one of the last surviving Dundee dynasties: celebrated for its hard professional training, family idiosyncrasies, and benevolent paternalism. Whereas other Dundee tycoons extracted their money from the city and mutated to country lairds, the Thomsons remain yet. Their flagship – *Courier & Advertiser* – derives from two opposing papers: the radical *Dundee Advertiser*, founded in 1801 to *establish a paper in which the liberal sentiments of the people could be freely expressed*, and the Conservative *Courier*, founded in 1816. The *People's Friend* and the *People's Journal* joined in the mid-19th century. The group is now as much famous for its comics, and characters such as Biffo the Bear, Oor Wullie, Desperate Dan, Lord Snooty, and the *Sunday Post*. Dennis the Menace now has an American television clone that entirely misses the point.

Courier Building as first built

Scottish features peculiar to that country in the 16th century ... The central portion was designed to Scott's intention, 1873, by David Mackenzie, and the **Eastern Galleries**, 1887, by the City Architect, William Alexander (colour page 52) Superb building, wonderfully restored: spectacular Renaissance horseshoe staircase affixed to the Gothic western façade. DDC Architects' restoration has revealed a masterpiece of rich polychromy, the stencils in the hall being rediscovered for the first time since 1887. The Galleries have been refurbished. Its splendid collection, now including the Orchar Collection, contains paintings by MacTaggart, Orchardson and Sargent. Statues around the outside include George Duncan (Dundee's first Reform MP) by Sir John Steell RA, James Carmichael (engineer father-in-law to Peter), and Robert Burns pensively contemplating D C Thomson's cultural empire to the west. Now commemorating Lord Provost Maurice McManus, the last stage in the rediscovery of this fine building would be to cease its isolation on a virtual traffic island, allowing its visitors to be mown down by roadrunners. A proposed pedestrianisation and landscaping deserves implementation.

18 **Courier Building**, 22 Meadowside, 1902, Niven & Wigglesworth
The gable of the headquarters of D C Thomson Ltd terminates Albert Square to the west. Thomson selected London architects, one of whose partners – David Niven – came from Angus, and the other had travelled to America to study the William Randolph Hearst empire. Upon early reinforced concrete foundations (only too necessary following the saga of the Exchange) arises a tall, confident, red stone, steel-framed office block in the American manner: gigantic pilasters reach through

several storeys as frame for the metal structure behind. Sculptures of Literature and Justice by Albert Hodge impose upon you as you enter from Meadowside. Notable American-inspired inter-war tower added 1960, as though it were original, by T Lindsay Gray. For aficionados of Desperate Dan, the Courier Building may be compared to architectural cow pie: delicious for those who like it.

High School Annexe (former Panmure Trinity Church), Panmure Street, 1855, David Bryce
Picturesque if demure church with Gothic rose window and flanking octagonal towers. The *Building Chronicle* liked the way that Bryce had introduced *nothing that did not perform a structural part in the design*. Well converted to library and hall, 1985, by Wellwood/Leslie Architects.

19 **Guardian Royal Exchange**, 1957, Gauldie Hardie Wright & Needham
Possibly the best 1950's building in Dundee: plainly elegant, dark plinth, three lighter storeys above with cornice and set-back

Top left *Original perspective of the Courier Building: immensely impressive American block dominating its lower scaled surroundings.* Top *Courier extension.* Above *Former Panmure Trinity Church.* Left *Guardian Royal Exchange*

Royal Exchange: perspective by David Bryce

The Royal Exchange Competition
Plans were sent to a number of architects throughout Scotland, the terms being that the usual commission would be given to the successful party. Some six or seven designs were sent in and were exhibited in the Baltic Coffee House. The directors selected two, but subsequent discussions having shown that neither of these could be adopted with anything like unanimity, it was resolved to compromise the matter by setting both aside. A commission was accordingly given to Mr Bryce of Edinburgh to prepare fresh plans and these having been approved of, the work was proceeded with. The directors, without any obligation to do so, gave 20 guineas to the authors of the two designs referred to above, understood to be Mr Burnet of Glasgow and Mr Maclaren of Dundee. The Building Chronicle, edited by one of the disappointed competitors, James Maclaren, watched in fascination as the new Exchange sank into the marsh of the Meadows: **July 1854**: *The nature of the foundations having been such as to require artificial means of security, Mr Bryce commenced with a layer of concrete 3 foot thick. The insufficiency of this is already too evident: the front wall being some inches off the perpendicular, the inside arches slacked, and the rents visible in various places.* **October**: *the sinking of foundations at the new Royal Exchange in Dundee has now become so serious that further operations on the Tower have been suspended.* **December**: *The Royal Exchange still stands in statu quo, an unfortunate object.* **June 1855**: *Signs of an attempt to complete the Tower are at length visible. We believe the ornate upper part is to be wholly omitted, and a peak roof substituted to finish it off with as little additional weight as possible.* **September**: *The Tower has been summarily stopped – we cannot say finished – with a pierced Gothic parapet immediately above the clock. The whole ornate spire contemplated in the original design is now sacrificed to the imperative prudence which forbids additional weight being put upon an insufficient foundation.*

dormered roof. Centre bays recessed behind columns and balconies. Unusual visual interest at a time of puritanism. (colour page 52)

RCAHMS

20 **Royal Exchange**, 1854–5, David Bryce Competition-winning design (third variant thereof) for the Dundee Chamber of Commerce symbolising that it had outgrown the Baltic Coffee House in the Cowgate. Its focus was the cavernous reading room with its open hammer-beam roof (now enclosed) and Cottier stained glass. Appropriately, Bryce's imagery was that of a Flemish Cloth Hall. The Reading Room's rank of tall ornamented dormer windows marched up to the squat base of the tower at the eastern end. It was designed to be surmounted by further stages and a swelling Flemish crown. Unfortunately Bryce miscalculated the foundations required for the marsh. The Exchange tilted, was secured with difficulty, and the tower became history. How splendid it would be for it to be completed now in lightweight materials, such as glass reinforced plastic, as a symbol of Dundee's regeneration.

The **Pizza Gallery** (former Union Bank), 1878, a three-storey Renaissance pile by Alexander Johnston lies across the road from his **11–13 Panmure Street**, 1892, with its giant Corinthian columns.

Cable Finance, 33 Albert Square, 1886, John Murray Robertson
A stern elegance to this former Caledonian Insurance building: twin bays rise to ornately

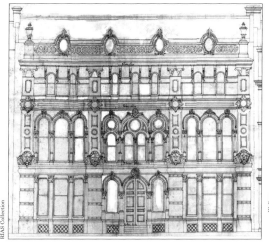

RIAS Collection

Left *Elevation of F T Pilkington's Eastern Club, Albert Square, demolished for unsuitability to conversion to bank.* Below *Exchange Reading Room.* Middle *Cable Finance.* Bottom *Cleghorn Housing Association*

Walker

sculptured parapet surmounted by pedimented double dormer with sunburst motifs and enfolding volutes. Almost American in its freedom with historic styles. Robertson had his own offices in these chambers.

21 **37 Albert Square** (former Prudential Building), 1875, Alfred Waterhouse & Son
Either Dundee, or age, was taming the exuberance of Waterhouse's Prudential buildings – so much more modest a version is this, than his English ones. *The Builder* disliked the *dull red brick that seems inevitable even in towns where stone is the usual and natural material* but found the design *quiet and pleasing.* The verticality of its skyline has been diminished by the removal of the tall arch-linked chimney stacks. Glazed tile interior by Paul Waterhouse. **Cleghorn Housing Association**, next door, 1975, Baxter Clark & Paul is neighbourly in dark brick: an urbane recognition of the importance of Albert Square which makes Waterhouse's design seem fanciful by comparison.

RIAS Collection

Pearl Building, Meadowside, 1898, Charles & Leslie Ower
The quarrelsome engineer/architect sons of the Harbour Engineer were responsible for some of Dundee's most distinctive houses. Much of the best detail here is from the hand of W G Lamond in red sandstone Flemish.
Meadowplace Buildings (former Jute Industries), 1886, James Maclaren, was once the headquarters of the mighty Cox Brothers, signalled by an appropriately grand porch of

Baxter Clark & Paul

India Buildings

RIAS Collection

Opposite: Top *Dundee, approaching from Fife, c.1845.* Middle right *Interior of St Paul's Cathedral.* Middle left *High Street looking west to the Union Hall & St Mary's Tower by George McGillivray, 1847.* Bottom *A wonderfully naïve painting by an unknown artist of Dundee from the river, c.1855*

J Murray Robertson, a strict Plymouth Brother, was to become one of Dundee's most distinctive architects. Brought to Dundee by Andrew Heiton when designing Castleroy (Broughty Ferry) for the Gilroy family, he so suited that they encouraged him to embark on practice on his own. Deeply influenced by Alexander Thomson, and then by America (particularly H H Richardson), Robertson experimented with the use of mass concrete and flat detailing. His leitmotif became projecting, flattened bays capped by ogee roofs. The practice became Robertson & Findlay, then Findlay, Stewart & Robbie, Robbie & Wellwood, to the Wellwood Leslie Partnership.

granite Corinthian columns and entrance mosaics. **Bonar House**, 1928, Robert Gibson (now used by the High School), was gifted to the city by George Bonar to provide business and management training.

India Buildings, 86 Bell Street, 1876, John Murray Robertson
Robertson's first solo Dundee commission – although small – may be taken as a homage to Alexander Thomson in Glasgow in its exemplification of architecture as decorated structure: precisely channelled stonework, predominantly glazed, and modulated by wide flat columns. Splendid pedimented entrance door with battered walls. **Mercantile Buildings**, 46–54 Bell Street, a red sandstone double-fronted commercial block has huge five-bay dormered windows.

Dundee College of Technology

RIAS Collection

Dundee College of Technology, 40 Bell Street, 1907
A curious tale. Competition for the façade won by School Board architect J H Langlands (W G Lamond's pencil evident in sinuous details and art nouveau-decorated glass) superimposed upon a standard plan design by Robert Gibson. Central pedimented entrance with flanking wings tuned up by overblown baroque. Distinctive boiler house chimney.

22 **High School**, Euclid Crescent, 1824, George Angus
The idea, entitled *Seminaries*, was to combine Dundee's Academy, Grammar School and the

John Gray

Dundee Museums & Art Galleries

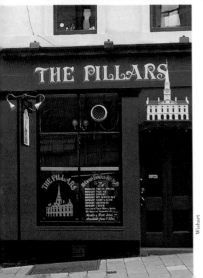

Wishart

Wishart

Top *Ceiling in 'Specsavers', Reform Street.* Middle *Dundee harbour & town looking eastwards on a summer's evening, c.1780 by an unknown artist.* Above *Caird Hall pillars in springtime.* Left *Model of the old Town House adorning 'The Pillars'*

Wishart

John Gray

John Gray

John Gray

T Lindsay Gray

Top left *RRS Discovery*. Top *The Unicorn*. Middle left *Interior of St Andrew's Kirk*. Above *Upper Dens*. Left *Elevation of the Calendar, March 1861*

Top right & top *External & internal stairs of the McManus Galleries.* Above *The Howff.* Right *Mercantile Bar, Commercial Street.* Below right *Guardian Royal Exchange & Albert Square – original perspective*

High School: Above *Drawn by Joseph Swan in the 1830's. Note Ward Road Congregational on the left.* Left *High School portico*

Kirkyard School into a single building. The consequence is Dundee's finest neoclassical monument well worthy of comparison to the former Royal High School, Edinburgh. Raising finance from a locally levied Ale and Beer Tax, the Town Council organised an architectural competition of the kind much in vogue in Edinburgh, between Archibald Simpson (Aberdeen), George Smith (designer of the Exchange Coffee House) and Angus. Upon winning, the latter was instructed to take advantage of his competitors' designs (which he certainly did of Smith's). Planned as the focus of the view up the new Reform Street, the High School is the only significant piece of *Beaux Arts* planning in Dundee: and the steadfast refusal to undertake any subsequent planning of that type has left the High School marooned in an educational enclave with none of the spatial context that would have been to its advantage. Although not part of Albert Square, it is contiguous to it. A giant eight-columned Doric portico dominates a single-storey façade terminated at each end by mildly mannered pilastered pavilions.

The amalgamation of three Dundee schools in one building led to an educational *disruption* in the Burgh as soon as the Dundee School Board claimed rights of appointment. To forestall a crisis, Baillie William Harris offered the School Board £10,000 for a different school (on condition that it respected the High School's independence) with which they built Harris · Academy (see p.91). Harris also gave the High School £20,000 topped by another great Dundonian benefactor, Sir William Ogilvy Dalgleish, partner of Peter Carmichael in Baxter Brothers.

Girls' High School: Top right *As originally built*. Above *Details from the entrance elevation*. Below right *The Tympanum*

23 Girls' High School, 1889, J G Fairley
One of the finest and most ornate of modern structures in the city ... [whose architectural style] may be described as a free rendering of the Italian Renaissance with high pitched ornamental roofs similar to those of the Tuileries in Paris. Florid Francophile stuff with the high sculptured attic favoured by American millionaires. Pretty grand hall, staircase illuminated by stained glass windows with full-length figures symbolising Art, Science & Literature. First-floor **Assembly Hall**, 52ft long, pilasters, garlanded capitals, cornice and panelled ceiling. A notable feature was the heating system: *to purify the atmospheric air drawn into the building from the soot always floating in the atmosphere of a city, it is made to pass through large frames covered with open canvas which intercept the floating particles of carbon.* The design was attributed to Bailie McCulloch, a civil engineer: but it was really by his ex-partner Fairley.

Dundee High School, Euclid Street, 1867 was designed by James Maclaren as a Gothic Savings Bank. **4 Euclid Crescent**, 1891, James Langlands, is a Gothic (former) Secession Kirk.

24 Regional Music Centre, 1a West Bell Street,
1840, James Black
Originally a church, this classical corner is
elegantly reticent: raised ground floor is
rusticated, upper storey pilastered with blind
panels, balustraded roof. Designed as terminal
feature of a never-completed terrace humbled
by the 1881 arrival of the **Curr Night Refuge**,
Ireland & Maclaren, and the (disused) **Parish
Council Chambers**, 1900, William Alexander,
City Architect. *No expense has been spared to
make the new offices creditable to the Council ...
the boardroom is to be a magnificent apartment,
well lighted and sumptuously fitted up.*

25 Sheriff Court, West Bell Street, from 1833,
George Angus & William Scott
Only the western screen wall and pavilion
(Governor's House) survives of Angus's original
grandiose concept of the courthouse as
centrepiece of a classical enfilade. The
imposing neoclassical temple, containing the
courthouse, the work of William Scott, followed
in 1863. Doric portico, pilasters, round-headed
windows redolent of mid-century Edinburgh
banks. Currently under refurbishment by
Nicoll Russell Studio. **Salvation Army
Hostel**, Court House Square, 1851, Charles
Edward, designed originally as an industrial
school, has affinities to a Tudor manor house:
two-tone stone, sharp gables and a thin tower
like an inflated manse. Edward rose from Clerk
of Works into architecture. Most work was
carried out by his partner T S Robertson after
c.1865.

Methodist Church, 15–19 Ward Road, 1866,
David Mackenzie
Painted rubble Gothic (which Mackenzie,
designer of the block between Rattray and
Nicholl Streets, also adapted to Presbyterian

Top *Regional Music Centre*. Middle
Sheriff Court. Above *Ceiling detail
Sheriff Court*

business chambers), incongruously converted to a (disused) double-level drinking den.

Foresters Halls, 1900, David Baxter: *the Foresters are to be congratulated on their pluck in entering upon so large an expenditure –* three halls, one accommodating 900 and the other two 300 each. Red sandstone towers frame an adventurously asymmetrical entrance. **1–7 Ward Road**, 1869, Charles Edward, the three-storey warehouses have an unusual arcaded ground floor. **Ward Road Congregational**, 1833, J Brewster, conceals a simple rectangular box behind a pretty façade of plasterer's perpendicular.

General Post Office, Meadowside, 1898, W W Robertson
French Renaissance ... of a very ornamental character, so they thought upon completion. So it is. The only concessions to internal function visible on the façade are the high arched windows of the ground floor office, and the under-scaled domed corner tower containing the staircase. Principal entrance flanked by Corinthian pillars surmounted by the winged figures symbolic of postal and telegraph departments.

Top *Foresters Halls*. Above *Ward Mills (demolished)*. Right *General Post Office*

Barrack Street Museum, 1911, James Thomson
Opened by Andrew Carnegie, who paid for it, as the Ward Road Library (Central Branch Library & Central Reading Room). His idea was to rescue the Albert Hall from the intrusion of newspapers to a place primarily intended for students. The first floor contained a News Room with massive reading desks *capable of accommodating a sufficient supply, not only of local journals but also of the principal representative Scottish, English and Irish newspapers*, a magazine room (with

Barrack Street Museum

Wishart

The Howff Tombstones, 16th- to
19th-century monuments,
sarcophagi and sacrament houses,
are notable for their quirkiness. A
19th-century volume detailing all
inscriptions then decipherable
resides in the McManus Galleries.
The Victorians claimed to spot the
following:

J.P.P.
Provost of Dundee
Hallelujah
Hallelujee

and:

Here lie I
Epity Pie
My husband
Twenty bairns
And I

certain tables set apart for publications used
principally by ladies), and the Juvenile Section
(the boys having their separate entrance from
Ward Road). There was also a sculpture court,
and a room devoted to pictures of old Dundee.
Imposing façade in London baroque *à la*
Thomas Archer (fashionably re-interpreted by
E A Rickards). Now home of Dundee's Natural
History collection.

The Howff, Barrack Street

Enclosed by high walls or railings, graced with
beautiful mature trees, overlooked by Victorian
monuments, and lined on one side by the
curving, cobbled Barrack Street, the Howff
epitomises the heart of old Dundee. In 1564,
Mary Queen of Scots granted the lands of the
Greyfriars north of the burgh boundary to the
Council for use as a graveyard, since that of
St Clement's had become overcrowded and
unsanitary (just as in Edinburgh: Greyfriars
replaced St Giles). The Howff earned its name

The Howff: Below *Drawing of the
arcading.* Bottom *As it is*

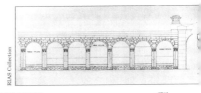

RIAS Collection

Dundee District Libraries

RIAS Collection

Above and right *Howff tombstones*

McKean

In 1825, a railroad was projected to connect Dundee with Newtyle, and in 1826 began to be constructed. It is now completely opened, and the coaches and waggons are employed to carry passengers and goods. The length of the railway is 11 miles and it cost upwards of £50,000. Leaving Dundee on the north, it ascends an inclined plane of about 800 yards in length and rising 1 yard in 10; at the top of this plane it is carried through a tunnel 340 yards in length to the north side of the Law of Dundee. There are two other inclined planes before reaching Newtyle. Up these planes, the carriages are drawn by means of fixed steam engines.
Trains were hauled uphill from the station in Ward Road by stationary steam engines at the top of the incline. The normal locomotive operated only on the plateau, supplemented as necessary by sails and horses.

Below *Newtyle Railway Station, Ward Road (demolished).* Bottom *The locomotive that operated on the plateau*

Dundee University Library

Dundee Art Galleries and Museums

(meeting place) from the curious fact that the Dundee Incorporated Trades' dealing floor was amongst these intimations of mortality. An outstanding collection of funerary monuments. The west wall retains huge, deep, blind arcading, 1601 (award-winning restoration carried out by DDC Architects) comparable to those that used to line Provost Pierson's mansion in the Greenmarket. Two curiosities: when built (and for a century or two thereafter), the Howff lay in the countryside; and the stone implies that the arcades may once have been open. It must therefore have been an unusually elegant abode of burial, at the head of the processional route from St Mary's along Friar's Wynd. (colour page 52)

Friarfield House, 1873,
James Maclaren and G S Aitken
Office block of the stunning (now demolished) Ward Mills, whose curious corner tower contains a circular entrance hall. Roof sliced off, French-style. **Willison House**, Willison Street, c.1934, Findlay Stewart & Robbie is a brash, faïence-faced furniture shop with art deco doorway: it must have looked much brighter in the days when this district was thriving. The west side of **North Lindsay Street** still presents a fine spectacle. The austere gigantic Halley Brothers, 1911, Harry Thomson, now offers flats with Venetian windows. The **Keyhole**, 1874, Maclaren & Aitken, was once part of the Lindsay Street Works. A mad, grotesquely over-exuberant French cathedral, with a steep-roofed oblong tower, whose tall gabled front with a rose window in the attic conveys a hint of St Denis, now flats for Hillcrest Housing Association, with a bar below. **Enterprise House**, 45 North Lindsay Street, c.1950 – a symmetrical brick

warehouse with brick detailed as stone –
converted to offices.

NETHERGATE

At the western end, Dundee's market place
bifurcated at the Luckenbooths. The older
route, the Overgate, ran north-west to the West
Port and out, west along Hawkhill to Perth,
north-west to Coupar Angus. The lower route
(originally Fleukergait, then Nethergate) led to
properties along the firth frontage. Only later
was it formalised to link the villages of
Westfield and Springfield, joining Perth Road
at the Sinderins. It retained its *aristocratic air*
until the mid-19th century, as the location for
the *elegant or flaunting homes of the elite*. Gaze
from the lounge of the **Queen's Hotel** and its
scale and majesty become apparent.

26 **City Churches (St Mary's Church,
Mary Slessor Centre & Old Steeple)**
St Mary's in the Field, 1442–3, replacing
that founded in thanksgiving by the Earl of
Huntingdon outside the city boundary, is by far
the largest non-cathedral church in Scotland.

Walker

City Churches: Left *In their
Nethergate setting: on the right,
Union Street, Whitehall Street and –
in the distance – the corner of
Crichton Street. Below City
Churches drawn by Joseph Swan
before the 1841 fire. Note the
unusual square-headed windows on
the right (which were also in the
gable) – almost certainly later 17th-
century*

RCAHMS

Old Steeple: Above *From the north.* Right *The main doorway. It is much changed today*

RIBA

Old Steeple, *c.*1460

Unmatched anywhere in the country, its nearest competitors – Stirling and Linlithgow – are pallid by comparison. From its tone, richness of carving and detail, we may infer something of the former Town's Churches, and of the wealth of the medieval mercantile community of Dundee – prior to 16th-century destruction by the *auld yenemies of England*, and obliteration by fire in 1841. Beautifully constructed of large blocks of varying coloured sandstone, the tower represented the burgh's completion of the largest medieval parish kirk in Scotland. It is divided into two stages by a cusped pinnacled parapet of lacy tracery: tower below, belfry above. Octagonal stair-tower in one corner. The groined vaulting within, the details of niches and buttresses, and the semi-circular oculus with its beautiful tracery bear witness to its quality. The pleasant tracery of its great western window above the door is a humane but much less elaborate version of the medieval original (embedded amidst flowers in Balgay Park). What we see is a careful recreation by Sir Gilbert Scott. The parapet indicates that a crown like St Giles was intended, but there is no certainty that it was built (it was not in place when Pont drew it in

Dundee Public Libraries

1592). The western entrance in its elegant stone frame is one of the finest in Scotland.

After the English burnt the nave in 1548, the Town left it derelict and converted transepts and choir into three separate churches, leaving the steeple free-standing in ruins. The **Steeple Church**, 1787, was built by Samuel Bell upon the site of the nave (originally called St Clement's Church) in a manner singularly lacking in conviction. Exiled to Dundee to recuperate in 1814–15, the satirist Thomas

Hood was tickled at four separate churches within one complex:
And four churches together with only one steeple,
Is an emblem quite apt for the thrift of the people.

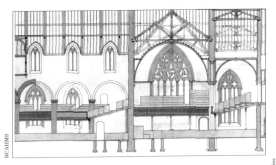

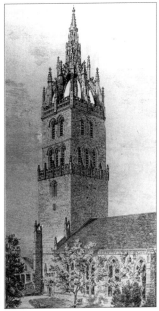

Above *Sir George Gilbert Scott's proposal to add a crown to the Old Steeple.* Left *Section through William Burn's St Mary's Church*

St Mary's Church

In 1841, a fire annihilated the church choir and transepts, witnessed by the architect James Maclaren: *Nothing could equal the frightful fury of the devouring element – it ran with the speed of lightning along the base, the galleries, the rafters of the church, at one moment a brilliant white line of light shot through the apex of the roof. After a moment of suspense, the flames burst with irresistible fury through the beautiful Gothic window facing the street in an intense mass of inconceivable brilliancy, carrying with it every portion of mason work ... About half past six the conflagration was at its height ... The crashing of the galleries as they yielded successively to the flames, the fall of ponderous roofs which shot volumes of fire into the air accompanied by dense clouds of embers – the sharp reports of stones splitting from walls and pillars resembling the discharge of artillery – and the frequent explosions which proceeded from the base of the buildings, contrived to create impressions of the most powerful and alarming character.* William Burn proposed to repair the churches, of which a substantial portion had survived – but unemployment in the building trade stimulated a lobby in favour of complete reconstruction (the same reason given for the death warrant of the Town House just 100 years later). Burn's polished Gothic – his plaster vaulting in the transepts (now the **Mary Slessor Centre**), and elegant St Giles – derived arcades and timber ceiling in the choir (now **St Mary's Parish Church**) – was as confident as the original. (colour page 69)

By proposing to reconstruct the Steeple's crown, Sir George Gilbert Scott outraged the celebrated architectural historian Dr Thomas Ross: *It is most lamentable to all who really take any practical interest in our national antiquities to find that nothing is safe from interference. The medieval architecture of Scotland is a closed chapter in our history, and we are not justified in altering or giving it an entirely different colour simply because we think it should have been something else, and it pleased the builders of the tower to finish it in the way we now behold. The fact remains that the architect of this tower had both [crown termination and a cape-house termination] before him as is shown by the indications left for finishing it with a crown form, and that he deliberately decided in favour of the cape-house. I believe the proposal now is to remove the cape-house and put up the dreadful design prepared by Sir G G Scott some 30 years ago. We have enough of his work in Scotland already.*

The Mercat Cross, a modern reproduction of the *Unicorn* by Scott Sutherland RSA surmounting John Mylne's 1586 carved shaft, is set in 1993 landscaping. The **Overgate Centre**, for which Dundee destroyed most of its surviving 17th-century heritage, may soon prove to be a transitory aberration as the city rediscovers the innate character of its spaces.

Couttie's Wynd, once a prominent thoroughfare to the harbour, survives as a back passage between Nethergate and Yeaman Shore – slightly rescued from its misery by a sculpture, 1991, by David Wilson.

27 **Debenhams** (formerly Draffen & Jarvie), 1935, Thoms & Wilkie
American-influenced steel-framed building whose stone facings are supremely elegant. Draffen & Jarvie were long-established Dundonian drapers whose celebrated tea room was panelled like an ocean liner. The design consists of a smart shopfront as plinth, surmounted by slender stone pilasters which rise up to the cornice, interrupted by a balcony. Attic storey beyond. Curious carvings on the cornice. Look closely at the windows and you will see how the stone is peeled back to reveal the metal frame behind. Draffen's success had gradually absorbed the entire west side of Whitehall Street, turning into this, its flagship building on the Nethergate.

28 **Whitehall Street** and **Crescent**, 1885–9, R Keith & others
Improvement Act clearance of a *narrow, steep, dingy and dirty* location *the courts and dark passages receptacles of filth ... always pervaded by offensive effluvia, sometimes so strong as to be sickening. It was in such localities that fever and death walked arm in arm, and contributed largely to the silent population of the Howff.* As

Above *Debenhams*. Top *Couttie's Wynd, alongside, drawn by David Small in the late 19th century.* Right *Whitehall Crescent*

in most Scots towns, history ceded to health. William Kidd, a Dundonian publisher, commissioned his friend Robert Keith to design the new street in *ornamental Gothic of a very handsome appearance*. Keith, a mason metamorphosed into a tenement designer, was a man of few design motifs – mostly Gothic. The *Dundee Year Book* was impressed: *large dwelling house blocks with shops have been finished within the year, and it speaks much for the central, convenient and breezy nature of the district near the docks that these houses should all have been taken up before or soon after they were completed. What a change! it might well be exclaimed by a visitor to Dundee who, returning after a few years' absence, could not help being struck with the enormous change in the amenities of Whitehall Crescent.* As in Commercial Street, the controlling design had been produced by the City Engineer, William Mackison, and his assistant, James Hutton.

Elevation of the Whitehall Street corner

Gilfillan Memorial Church, c.1890: the cupola is currently missing

Gilfillan Memorial Church, 1887, Malcolm Stark

Terminating the vista as centrepiece of Whitehall Crescent, the church has a square, worldly elevation, symmetrically disposed with vigorous baroque details around the door and windows. Flanked on either sides by shops, you would never know that this was a church. It is probably apposite for the subject: the notable Revd George Gilfillan, as celebrated for fights and controversies as for preaching, was a social reformer, partly responsible for the establishment of the asylum at Hawkhead, Paisley, and friend of William McGonagall.

The lanes and even several streets are uncommonly narrow, and the dwellings of the inhabitants too close upon one another; the greatest part of the families living by half dozens, as formerly in Edinburgh, under the same roof with common stairs, without backyards or courts, and many possessing only single rooms. The late additional suburbs have been built without any additional plan, and without the least regard to health, elegance or cleanliness; though no situation perhaps in the world presented better opportunities to provide for all the three.
Robert Small, First Statistical Account, 1793.

Editor of a sumptuous two-volume set of the works of Robert Burns, had he been alive today, he would have been a television pundit. His following was enormous, and his Memorial Church appropriately lavish (timber cupola contemplating resurrection by Simpson & Brown).

Property Centre, 9 Whitehall Crescent, refurbished 1989, Ritchie Dagen & Allan
An amazing case of retrofit. Rescued from behind an ungainly 1960's fascia was a late 19th-century Quaker Meeting House, complete with lettering. Award-winning conversion has restored the curved glass, exposed the iron columns and splendid timber doorway, and has retained the internal lacy gallery balcony (painted red) for upper level house-selling.

Right *Property Centre, Whitehall Crescent as rediscovered.*
Right below *Union Street c.1880 before the Royal Hotel alterations. The Thistle Hall visible two-thirds way up.* Below *Union Street after James Maclaren's transformation for the Royal Hotel*

29 **Thistle Hall**, 11–19 Union Street, 1828, David Neave
Union Street followed William Burn's 1824 recommendations for new streets – four-storey stone buildings of shops with handsome flats above. Some retain their plasterwork and panelling. The Dundonian stone now looks somewhat frayed and all that survives of the Thistle Hall are its grand windows and Ionic

pilasters, which James Maclaren incorporated into his flamboyant Royal Hotel, 1880.

Nethergate Centre, 1975, Hugh Wilson & Lewis Womersley
The scale of this enclosed centre is more like an arcade linking Nethergate, through the medieval long riggs, to Yeaman Shore. Almost invisible in its reticence, its architecture is of crisp masonry-like blockwork, symmetrically placed windows, and an elegant mansard roof. The rear of adjacent Nethergate buildings displays historic fragments and traces of their wonderful predecessors.

30 **Mecca** (formerly Green's Playhouse), 1936, John Fairweather with Joseph Emberton
Rare survivor of Dundee's 28 cinemas, and probably the largest bingo hall in the world, Green's with seats for 4117 was a symbol of Dundonian celluloid fever. (The city had a cinema for every 6007 inhabitants; Glasgow a poor second with one for every 8400, Edinburgh one for every 9675, and Aberdeen one for every 11,854.) The somewhat dull Fairweathers were good at speedy, huge volume auditoria; but they needed pep. Green imported Joseph Emberton, fresh from Blackpool, to design the stylish tower (with its squint *U*) and fashionable foyer/restaurant. The restaurant normally catered for 160 people, but at weekends it doubled its capacity by colonising the foyer. Emberton's finned tower survives beneath its cloak of grey ribbed metal. Unbelievably introduced to bring the cinema's image more up to date, it has the opposite effect, and the tower should be returned to its original pzazz. John Alexander of Newcastle was consultant for the wondrous Corinthian-columned auditorium – pure American classic.

Meadowside St Paul's, Nethergate, 1850, Charles Wilson
Of no great merit claimed *The Builder*, yet the tall thin spire of this church marches well with Green's tower next door, and its Gothic Revival façade (flanked by original shops) lends quality and interest to the locality. Hall extension, 1989, by Reid & Greig. The only good thing to say about the destructive Ring Road is how the Art Project has ameliorated the damage: curved handrails, David Wilson's *Wave Wall*, and Brian Snell and John Gray's transformation of the previously squalid

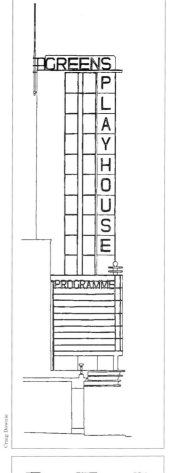

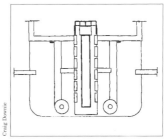

Original elevation and plan by Joseph Emberton of Green's Playhouse advertising tower

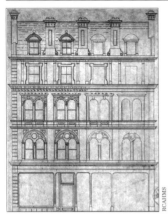

Above *132–134 Nethergate.* Right
*Proposal for Marketgait opposite by
Nicoll Russell.* Below *Miln's
Buildings.* Below right *St Andrew's
Cathedral*

Nethergate Underpass. Pavement mosaics,
1991, by Elizabeth McFall.

132–134 Nethergate, 1873, Young & Meldrum
A corner building against its will, flank naked to
the Ring Road, upmarket tenement building for
Provost Don embellished with Venetian first-floor
windows and elegant chimney stacks.
Flamboyant corner building opposite by the Nicoll
Russell Studio yet to materialise. Marketgait
requires to be bridged, perhaps re-using relics
from the demolished St Enoch's Church.

31 **Miln's Buildings**, 136–140 Nethergate, *c.*1790,
Samuel Bell
Crudely detailed speculative mansion flats
built by James Miln with bows facing the firth.
The only such development of this antiquity in
Dundee, it would repay reconditioning. **St
Andrew's Roman Catholic Cathedral**, 150
Nethergate, 1835, George Mathewson, is more

Within these last 40 years *Dundee
has been much improved – new and
spacious streets have been opened –
narrow lanes have been removed –
and in the place of old shabby
houses there have been built many
substantial dwellings. There are
several large and handsome halls,
and amongst the modern buildings
are to be noticed the Royal
Infirmary, the Royal Lunatic
Asylum, a splendid coffee room, and
there is, in the course of being built,
an elegant Academy.*
Second Statistical Account, 1833.

like a chapel than a cathedral: somewhat unconvincingly perpendicular pinnacled gable facing the street in what *The Builder* dismissed as *churchwarden's Gothic*. Surprisingly impressive within, arcades dividing the space into three bays, focusing upon C J Menart's mystical apse, 1921. (colour page 70)

Clydesdale Bank (former Nethergate House), 158 Nethergate, 1790, possibly Samuel Bell
Originally Nethergate House, seat of power of the celebrated Provost Alexander Riddoch, who controlled the burgh virtually single-handedly (so his opponents claimed) for almost 40 years until he lost office in 1819 following his defeat over the Harbour Bill. Surprisingly unpretentious for such an alleged demon of corruption, the house is plain, elegant, graced by an Ionic doorway and slightly bowed windows. Single-storey symmetrically placed pavilions on either side, perhaps incorporating parts of the Town's Hospital formerly on the site.

One artful and ambitious individual. Historians are ambivalent about the morality of Alexander Riddoch, Provost of Dundee, 1789–1819. *A ketteran bit callan* when he first appeared from Comrie, he amassed sufficient gear to become Laird of Blacklunans and Treasurer of (and money lender to) the Town. His level head in controlling the riots during the Revolutionary period, and his modernisation of the town, attracted admiration. However, his ruthless control of the Council for almost 40 years, and several dubious land transactions where the Council subsequently required to build, fuelled allegations of corruption, to the extent of satirical songs:
*Sell'd himsel stances, grew rich and his creatures
Set up o'er the natives
o' Bonnie Dundee.*
A petition was placed before Parliament in 1819 for the reform of the Town's governance. Riddoch's real fault, as stated by W Norrie, was that *his management of the town's revenues had been characterised as niggardly rather than judicious, and it has been questioned whether due means were employed to increase the income as well as keep down the expenditure of the Corporation*. It was Riddoch's sturdy individualism and distaste of corporate action that meant that Dundee – almost alone of all significant Scots towns – enjoyed barely a whisper of the neoclassical town planning and monuments that represent one of Scotland's principal architectural glories.

Lord Cockburn, probably influenced by the Riddoch saga, could believe only the worst of Dundee. In 1844, he referred (in *Circuit Journeys*) to *Dundee, that palace of Scottish blackguardism, un'...*

Left

Above *Queen's Hotel*. Right *Morgan Tower*

Queen's Hotel, Nethergate, 1878,
Young & Meldrum
This hotel was to be Dundee's riposte to
Edinburgh's North British; so it marks the
kink in the Nethergate by a thumping French
confection with huge chimneys, a three-storey
dormer roof, two storeys of vaguely Gothic
windows and a chamfered corner. *The Builder's*
comment that it was *as Gothic as pointed
arches to the windows, recessed with little
columns in them, and wooden bargeboards to
the dormers can make it* was less than
generous. It is less Gothic than commercial
with spiky overtones, like a *Mairie* in Alsace.
Quality (mutilated by Fire Officer) within –
splendid oaken staircase, opulent first-floor
lounge overlooking the Nethergate with
exceptional plasterwork and coffered ceiling.
Civic arms on the dining room ceiling imply
institutional support.

The Queen's Hotel is an object
lesson to architects wishing to
become developers. Acting upon
privy information that the new
Caledonian Station would be at
Seabraes, Young & Meldrum built
this hotel as Dundee's principal
station hotel. Their inside
information was misconceived. The
company took its terminus
further into town, and the
hotel proved financially
disastrous. Andrew Mackie
assisted as assistant in
the group.

Morgan Tower, 135–179 Nethergate, 1794
Immensely solid block of mansion flats in the
manner of Samuel Bell, notable for the five-
storey bow which projects into the street
providing Dundee's only townscape experience

RMJM

McKean

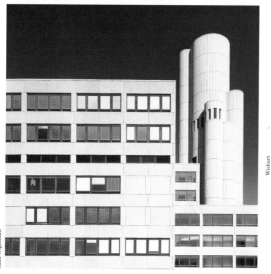

Alan Wightman

Wishart

Top *Botanic Gardens Visitors'
Centre*. Above *Nyoora*. Top left
*Ninewells Hospital, Invergowrie &
Tay Valley from the air. Invergowrie
House in the trees, centre left.* Left
Ninewells Hospital

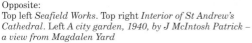

Opposite:
Top left *Seafield Works*. Top right *Interior of St Andrew's Cathedral*. Left *A city garden, 1940, by J McIntosh Patrick – a view from Magdalen Yard*

Top *Geddes Quadrangle, University of Dundee*. Above *Intervention by Nicoll Russell in the College of Art*. Above right *Inside Pennycook Court*. Right *Students' Association*

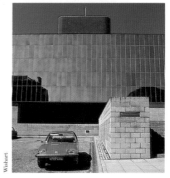

Top *Ceiling detail of the hall,
The Vine.* Middle *Magdalen Green
bandstand.* Above *David Neave's
original elevation for Tay Street.*
Top right *Interior of St Mary's Kirk.*
Right *Bonar Hall*

of the kind. It would be even more striking if the harling that would have concealed the rubble were reinstated. The tower is pierced by a column of wonderfully vulgar Venetian windows, and capped by an ogee roof like a saracen's hat, with a Muslim moon as weathervane. Wanchancy tradition had it that these oriental features were at the request of a sea captain owner called Morgan. In reality, it was built as a speculation by Daniel Morgan of Westfield. Yet the thickness of the walls, the huge blocks of red sandstone, the well to the rear, and the curious U-shape building behind the adjacent terrace imply that this 18th-century speculation may well have utilised earlier structures. Restored as flats, 1990, for Cleghorn Housing Association by the Parr Partnership.

South Tay Street, 1819–29, David Neave
Laid out in 1792 through the grounds of the Town's Hospital to join Hawkhill to Nethergate. Mostly constructed some 20 years later by Neave, who lived there, the east side comprises

Drawing of the Morgan Tower

We, the Provost, Bailies, Council, Deacons of Crafts in the commonality of the burgh of Dundee ... by these present, dispone perpetually to the Masters of the Hospital or Almshouse of this burgh and successive Masters thereof, in the name of the poor which shall be placed therein to, all and the whole of the foresaid places, yards, crofts, and acres of land with all and sundry gear pertaining, which pertain to the said Greyfriars, Blackfriars, Grey Sisters, and now to us by reason of the disposition thereof.
Dundee Charters, 1569–70

Left *South Tay Street c.1900.* Below left *Firth of Tay, South Tay Street in the foreground.* Below *House in South Tay Street remodelled by C & L Ower*

the city's best-surviving classical terrace.
Pleasant three-storey houses in Dundee's poor
stone, lacking the raised, rusticated ground
floors of Edinburgh streets. Pleasant ironwork
balconies, Ionic pilastered or columned
doorways, and a good fanlight window or two.
Looks chipper following restoration. (colour
page 69)

32 **Dundee Rep Theatre**, Tay Square, 1982,
Nicoll Russell Studio
Award-winning bravura modern composition
comprising a large rectangle in light concrete
blockwork whose façade is punctured to reveal
the inside to the outside. A cantilevered
staircase which winds up to the first-floor
gallery penetrates the glazed screen; and this
merging of inside and outside is carried through
by gravel on both sides. To contrast with the
bright blocks and green transparency of glass,

Top right *South Tay Street*. Top
*Palais de Danse doorway, Tay
Street*. Above *David Neave's
drawing for a door at the centre of
Tay Street*. Right *Dundee Rep
Theatre*

the architects have deployed dark stained timber poles, triangles and boarding. Once within the glass screen, all front-of-house spaces are interlinked in a circuitous route providing a sequence of various spaces each with its own character – restaurant, sitting area, bar, foyer and gallery. The superstructure was extended south-west, in like manner, 1990, by the DDC Architects (Colin Wishart) to provide rehearsal room and ancillary facilities. Adjacent **Doctors' Surgery**, and flats, 1992, Blaikie Johnston Withers, missed the opportunity of completing the formality of the Square.

Above *Dundee Rep Theatre extension.* Left *Rehearsal room*

162–172 Nethergate line the cliff edge of the Tay, all late 18th century, contiguous, cramped, wealthy merchants' houses – mostly extended; **164**, 1785, (?)Samuel Bell, has a Venetian doorway; **166**, 1818, David Neave, has a projecting central bay with an exuberantly rolling keystone above the delicate fanlight. **Caird House**, **172**, 1840, has an Ionic porch, and handsome balustrade. The adjacent late 18th-century house retains its original kitchen/scullery.

Grange House, Nethergate: north façade, 1817, David Neave

Geddes Quadrangle & Carnegie Building

Patrick Geddes, 1854–1932
The Geddes Quadrangle, built in 1909, commemorates Sir Patrick Geddes, part-time Professor of Botany at University College, Dundee 1889–1919. A Chair was created especially for him which allowed Geddes to spend nine months of his year in Edinburgh, London, Paris, Cyprus, USA, India and Palestine. With this freedom, he created his travelling *Cities* exhibition which was launched in Edinburgh. The exhibition not only established Geddes' reputation as a planner, but was seminal in the founding of the discipline of Town Planning. He was subsequently commissioned to study planning aspects of some 50 cities worldwide.

University of Dundee

Dundee's College was founded in 1881 to prepare students for external degrees for the University of London. In 1897, it became part of the University of St Andrews, bearing the title of University College, Dundee – largely the result of a £120,000 bequest from Miss Baxter. In 1967, it became the University of Dundee. In 1888, the Technical Institute – again upon Baxter munificence (that of Sir David) – was established in neighbouring Small's Wynd. The College began by utilising villas of the elegant Regency suburb of Hawkhill, and expanded gradually to digest Park Place, Small's Wynd, Park Wynd, Airlie Place and now, with its ingestion of the College of Art, Hawkhill Place and Springfield. Here and there survive villas engulfed by departments, and overshadowed by monuments.

Union Mount, 1813, and **Ellenbank**, 1808(?), David Neave, are two substantial two-storey

Right *Union Mount & Ellenbank – now University Departments*. Below *Bonar Hall*

villas with projecting central bays, one pedimented, and the other with a substantial
33 portico. **Bonar Hall**, Park Place, 1975, Gillespie Kidd & Coia, is a quality arrival in lurid orange brickwork and dark boarding – planned originally as part of a larger complex to include the theatre. Chunky, set low in the site, and emphatically horizontal, the two foyers within are joined by an elegant neo-Mackintosh staircase (colour page 69).

Scrymgeour Building, Park Place, 1911–12, T M Cappon, built as a training college, is red sandstone institutional Renaissance similar in scale and form (if not detail) to the Institute of Art & Technology. It would have been much more impressive if facing open land as was
34 originally intended. **Tower Building**, 1957–8, Robert Matthew Johnson-Marshall & Partners, contains administration, continuing education, some arts, and social science room. Unobtrusive, as towers go, in dark boarding

RIAS Collection

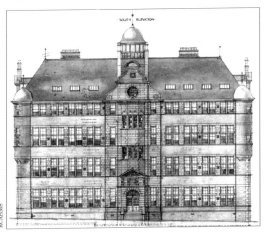

RCAHMS

Dundee University Library

and stone, with a largely glazed podium. **Old Medical School** facing a short, narrow lane, was sketched out by J Murray Robertson and built by his successor James Findlay. Its vigour can only be appreciated in elevation: like a French château modified by Chicago – dominant central entrance capped by curvilinear gable with volutes and cupola, corner domed turrets. Original tiered lecture theatres with original panelling within. The
35 **Old Technical Institute**, Small's Wynd, 1886, also by Robertson, captures the eye for its combination of square severity and shallow detail, some picked out in different coloured stone. A distinctively inventive design of very

Top *Scrymgeour Building*. Left *Old Medical School*. Above *Tower Building*

thin detail, curious entrance capped by three arched windows, and didactic sculptured panels.

Geddes Quadrangle/Carnegie and Harris

36 **Buildings** 1907, Rowand Anderson & Paul
The heart of the campus, a small part of a more grandiose University concept by the same architects. The quality makes one regret the larger brother was never built. In deep red stone with originally buff dressings, the Harris (Physics) Building is an energetic variation of late 17th-century Scots architecture with a large tolbooth tower to the rear, possibly implying the hand of Balfour Paul rather than Anderson. Invention and detail of the Carnegie Building is stunning: best appreciated by its pedimented southern gable in which a Venetian window is irreverently granted bull's-eyes. The quadrangle, a sundial at its centre, elegiac and memorable of late 17th-century Scotland, is named after Sir Patrick Geddes, once Professor of Botany, who transformed this space into a Teaching Garden. (colour page 71)

Above right *Old Technical Institute.*
Top *Carving from the old Technical Institute.* Above *Gable of the Carnegie Building.* Below *Carnegie Building*

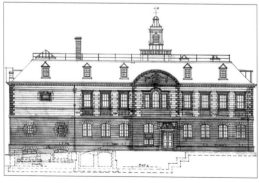

37 **Belmont Hall**, 1963,
Gauldie Hardie Wright & Needham
Quadrangular hall of residence, a tower in one

RIAS Collection

corner, one wing perched on thin piloti and good, hard, Scandinavian landscaping. Much influenced by contemporary development in Denmark, it represented *the last flicker of the belief that some introduction to graceful living was a function of University education.* The **Medical Sciences Institute**, 1970, Mackie Ramsay & Taylor, a muscular medieval fortress in white concrete, is supported upon splayed legs.

Airlie Place, 1851, J Dick Peddie
Smart short stone terrace of excellent neoclassical detail now amalgamated into the **Airlie Hall of Residence**. The **Students' Association**, 1970, James Parr & Partners, closes the top with a refined smooth glass-walled box above a red brick plinth. A sophisticated if unsubtle way of enclosing bars, meeting rooms and game rooms. The

McKean

Top *Belmont Hall: original perspective.* Above *Medical Sciences Institute.* Below *Feuing plan for Airlie Place.* Bottom *Students' Association (colour page 71)*

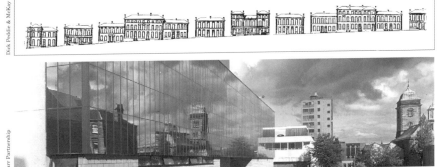

Dick Peddie & McKay

Parr Partnership

79

University Library, Peters Lane, 1985–6, by Faulkner Browns consists of two upper storeys clad in vertical precast concrete above a largely glazed plinth. **Seabraes Gentlemen's Lavatory**, 40 Perth Road, William Mackison, is green and white tiled, with a mosaic floor and original brass fittings.

38 Duncan of Jordanstone College Crawford Building, 1937, James Wallace Competition-winning scheme delayed by the Second World War, and completed in 1950 to a changed design. Large brick rectangle whose south façade is boxed out largely in glass. Jazzy interventions by Nicoll Russell Studio within – glass blocks, curved walls, metal staircases and primary colours. The forecourt requires similar attention. (colour page 71)

Above *Seabraes Gentlemen's Lavatory*. Below *View of the College of Art*. Bottom *Matthew Building*

39 Matthew Building, 1974, Baxter Clark & Paul

Confident Brutalist architecture for a School of Architecture whose interior quality is as good as can be found elsewhere for the period in Scotland. Subtle use of the concrete frame allows views from one floor to the next, deep lightwells, a sense of contrasting spaciousness and enclosure. A good example of how modern materials can provide a sense of light and volume within even the most complex building. A ceiling from Carbet Castle (see p.151) is mummified within the hall at an inebriated angle. **School of Television & Imaging**, 1992, Wellwood Leslie, is perched high within – glass, glass block floors, primary colours appropriate for a European leader in imaging technology.

THE WESTERN APPROACH

One of the finest entrances to any city in Britain, **Perth Road** runs along the sea ridge, lined on both sides by great houses, mature trees, stone walls, or fine terraces, comprising an asset that would be difficult to price. After quitting the University, it passes through a compact, principally 18th-century shopping street to break out into Victorian villadom at the **Sinderins**, the junction of Hawkhill and Blackness Avenue. **Blackness Road**, a contour higher, winds a parallel route around the south edge of Balgay Hill. The greater houses were those nearer the water's edge, becoming smaller as they rose.

FIRST SUBURB:

Roseangle/Magdalen Yard was a low-lying peninsula penetrating the Tay before the firth's shoreline was extended by successive reclamation for the Esplanade, the railway, the bypass and the airport. Its name may recollect medieval monastic connections, for the Victorians recorded the discovery of carved stones at the foot of Step Row. Dundee's first self-contained suburb, its villas spread down Roseangle to the Yard (colour page 71). The steep slope down from Perth Road eventually became crowded with poorer housing and industry, and a fatal blow to the suburb's privileged status was the arrival of the railway,

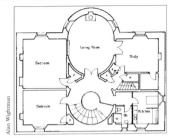

Above Plan of Hawkhill House *(demolished for the Matthew Building).* Below *Magdalen Green bandstand from MacFarlane's Catalogue.* Bottom *St John's Church.* Bottom left *Roseangle*

William McGonagall (to himself Sir William Topaz McGonagall, Knight of the White Elephant of Burma) was the world's most celebrated bad poet. A handloom weaver in a mill up the Scouring Burn until made redundant by the introduction of machinery, he taught himself from a set of *penny Shakespeares* (which accounts for his archaisms). Retreating to a lair in Paton's Lane, he became a populist poet, prepared to address any evening in the manner of 17th-century popular Bab Sheets and Balladists. Dispensing with poetical tools such as rhythm and structure, McGonagall's verses were created around rhyme and the cadences of dramatic recitation, in a popular idiom appropriate to his audience. McGonagall had a sad life, dominated by poverty and derision. Of the latter, the cruellest examples were the purchase for him of a one-way ticket to America, and a presentation of his portrait in oils – a photograph floating in a sardine can.

Below *The ill-fated first Tay Bridge: High Girders at the centre*. Bottom *The second Tay Bridge*

and the mutation of the firth's edge at Seabraes into marshalling yards. **The Green** was formed into a public park by Provost Alexander Lawson in the early 1840s, as a project to relieve the severe unemployment caused by *dull trade*, and the consequent threat from Chartists. By 1879, Magdalen Green had become *a place of resort much frequented by the west enders, for cricket and other games*. Its fine cast-iron **Bandstand**, 1890, is MacFarlane's design No 225 – the only other one of which is in Calcutta. Beautifully restored, 1991, by DDC Architects (J Oswald). (colour page 69)

40 **St John's Roseangle–Ryehill Church**, 1884, James Hutton
A striking Gothic silhouette with high quality details (fine organ case, 1895, R & J Sibbald) beckons downhill to Roseangle and a remembrance of Dundee's past: small Regency villas set into the hillside, classical porch to the street, lacy verandas overlooking all the gardens below that were once washed by the sea. Even now the view (particularly with glass in hand) over trees, railway, shore to the firth and the Tay Bridge, is elegiac, continental in feel, and distinctively under-appreciated.

41 **The (second) Tay Bridge**, 1886, W H Barlow & Crawford Barlow
One of the most gigantic works of mankind, the first Tay Bridge was designed by Sir Thomas Bouch as a single-track, lattice girder bridge finished in 1878. Unfortunately, a combination of poor inspection, faulty castings, insufficient allowances for wind pressure, and racing trains took their toll. An exceptional gale on 28 December 1879 blew down its High Girders at the centre, along with the 5.27pm passenger train from Burntisland. The replacement **Bridge**, with ironwork by Sir William Arrol, was completed at just under double the cost of the original whose designer, the unfortunate Sir Thomas Bouch, was by then dead.

2 **Magdalen Green** is of great but faded quality: substantial classical villas inter-mixed with industry and punctuated by tenements whose street names recollect a lost arcadia – **Greenfield**, **Westfield**, **Seafield**, **Bellfield**, **Shepherd's Loan** and **Strawberry Bank**. Most villas are substantially similar, in the manner of David Neave – two-storey stone houses, occasionally embellished with a projecting central bay, pediment, columns flanking the entrance, roof projections, fanlights or balconies. Most have mature, dank stone-walled gardens which define the street.

Magdalen Place, laid out 1836, George Mathewson
Short cul-de-sac, rather too tightly laid out, forming only coherent development of late classical villas, most with Doric columns or pilasters about their entrances.

3 **The Vine**, 43 Magdalen Yard Road, 1836, (?)W M Mackenzie (colour page 69)
Exceptional villa of national importance in late Regency mode. Designed as an art-gallery house for the art collector George Duncan MP (he who, by the magnificence of his court dress, upstaged the entire Town Council on the arrival of Queen Victoria in 1844). A square neo-Greek pavilion set upon a plinth within its garden, with fine views to the firth; incised stonework, spreading windows and a projecting entrance. There are significant similarities to Thomas Hamilton's Arthur Lodge (see *Edinburgh* in this series). The plan is focused upon a dome-lit hall with paired Ionic columns

Celebrations attending the opening of the Tay Bridge. The piper is dancing over swords bearing the mottos 'perseverance' and 'engineering skill'

When the December 1879 gale blew down the High Girders, McGonagall rushed to print:
Beautiful Railway Bridge of the Silvery Tay
Alas! I am very sorry to say
That ninety lives have been taken away.
(by, *inter alia*, the Demon of the Air, Boreas, and the loud brayings of the Storm Fiend)
I must now conclude my say
By telling the world fearlessly without the least dismay
That your central girders would not have given way
At least many sensible men do say
Had they been supported on each side with buttresses ...
When the new bridge was complete, McGonagall was satisfied with its structure:
Beautiful new railway bridge of the Silvery Tay
With your strong brick piers and buttresses ...

The Vine: Left Drawn by David Walker. Below Capitals in the hall. Bottom South elevation

Right *Garden façade of The Vine.*
Below *Elevation and plan of The Shrubbery by David Neave*

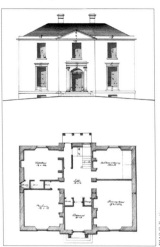

RIAS Collection

John Gray

in the corners; superb inlaid doors. Mackenzie was a Perth architect who, along with his brother Thomas, was responsible for its Infirmary in York Place.

The **Institute for the Blind**, 1883, Alexander Johnston, spreads between Paton's Lane and Step Row – large in bulk, small-scaled in detail. Tudor Collegiate with poorhouse overtones.

65 Magdalen Yard Road, one of a pair with **The Shrubbery**, **67**, were both designed *c*.1817, by David Neave
Pedimented central bay, and Ionic-columned doors, pavilion roofs, conservatory and wrought-iron lamps. **22**, **41** and **61** Magdalen Yard Road are similar.

Seafield Works, 1861, Robertson & Orchar
Soaring above its neighbourhood, Thomson & Shepherd's patterned-brick towered mill has been converted to flats with a leisure/ swimming complex by Baxter Clark & Paul (colour page 70).

Below *Seafield Works before conversion.* Right *Early sketch of the conversion proposals*

McKean

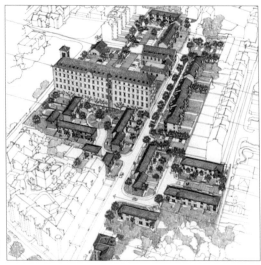

Baxter Clark & Paul

1-6 Windsor Place

RCAHMS

1–6 Windsor Place, 1835–40
Graceful neoclassical terrace of two-storey
stone houses, topped by a continuous
balustrade. The centre and the wings project
slightly. The rhythm of Doric-columned porches
is designed to achieve symmetry for the entire
terrace – the central houses having their
porches twinned into a single portico.

Below *Windsor Street.* Bottom *The Gate Fellowship*

RCAHMS

1–28 Windsor Street, 1872, James Maclaren
Splendidly confident terrace of houses running
downhill from Perth Road, of the sort that you
see in Brighton, save that Dundee stone has
greater majesty than Brighton stucco: pleasing
proportions, good Renaissance details on doors
and windows, and balustraded skyline.

150 Perth Road, 1790(?), Samuel Bell
When first built it must have been in the
country. Heavily restored, curiously urban
two-storey villa with Venetian window.

Gate Fellowship (former St Mark's Church),
158 Perth Road, 1868–9, Pilkington & Bell
Much of the hard-edged vividness that
characterises Pilkington. Two-tone stone
church on a corner site, façades in heavily
articulated Germanic detail that springs to life
in the afternoon sun. U-plan gallery with
twisted barley-sugar columns, hammer-beam

RCAHMS

85

Right Gate Fellowship: original interior. Below *Detail from the Speedwell Bar.* Below right *Springfield.* Bottom *Ryehill Church & Perth Road before decapitation*

roof carried on cast-iron columns. Addition by Ireland & Maclaren, 1879.

Speedwell Bar, 165–7 Perth Road, 1903, John Bruce & Son
Unspoilt Edwardian interior with art nouveau etched glass and lustrous woodwork, plasterwork and panelling.

2–32 Springfield, 1828
Regency terraced houses with Greek Doric porticos crowned by balustrades. **Ryehill Church**, 1878, George Shaw Aitken, presents an overblown gabled façade to the street with a florid tracery window. Converted to flats by CJFP Architects, 1987.

Whitetop Centre, Westfield Avenue, 1993, Nicoll Russell Studio
Centre designed for a multiple client to maximise the beneficial effects of design in all its aspects on profoundly handicapped people and on all their senses.

St Peter's Church, St Peter's Street, 1836, Hean Brothers
Remarkably douce for a revivalist kirk: yet this was the seat of the Revd Robert McCheyne

(1813–43), a major player in the Evangelical revival, who made these sober rafters ring. An elegant classical god-box, gallery within carried on cast-iron columns. Proportions and plain simplicity ennobled by the tower and stone spire against its east gable. Spire with oculi (like John Adam in Banff and John Baxter in Fochabers), the upper stages of the tower formally pedimented and pilastered. The **Mural**, Ryehill Lane, 1982, depicts the history of Dundee by the Edinburgh Artists Collective.

45 **Pennycook Court**, Pennycook Lane, 1986, Page & Park (colour page 71)
One of the best 20th-century buildings in Dundee. Winner of a 1986 architectural competition by the SSHA for architects under the age of 35, it consists of a corner tenement block with houses and wardens' houses uphill enfolding its own private and sun-filled courtyard – trellis, flowers, etc. Two-tone blockwork, projecting bays, shallow curved metal balconies, and clerestorey running beneath overhanging eaves – offering magnificent views to the Tay. Corner emphasised by chimneyed gable with common room at the bottom. Harmony lies in proportion and the modelling: detail is spare. An object lesson in contemporary urban infill. **Hawkhill School**, 1892, J H Langlands, opposite has Renaissance-derived details, balustrade and oversized urns. Amidst tenements and industry uphill, **Annfield**

Top *St Peter's Church*. Above *Interior*. Top left *Pennycook Court*. Left *Annfield House*

House, 5 Annfield Street, 1793, moulders quietly. One of Dundee's earliest classical suburban houses, its amenity encroached on all sides, it has a shallow south-facing three-bay bow lined, like a garter, with a lacy cast-iron balcony. Splendid if restored. The severe, late-Victorian tenements in **Peddie Street** have been humanised and rehabilitated by City Architects and Bell & Farquharson.

Below Gate Fellowship, north elevation. Right Interior, McCheyne Memorial Church

⁴⁶ **McCheyne Memorial Church**, 328 Perth Road, 1872, Pilkington & Bell Evangelical revival made manifest and with the best architect for the job. In Pilkington's idiosyncratic manner, an off-centre Germanic Gothic tower, incised stonework, with skilful galleried auditorium within.

St John's Cross Church

St John's Cross Church, Blackness Avenue, 1911–14, Frank Thomson
Heavyweight Romanesque, inscrutable cruciform church (lacking spire) of the Peter MacGregor Chalmers type. Symbolised one of Dundee's oldest and most influential congregations (the Cross Church, burnt out of the Town's Churches in 1841, moving to the Gaelic Chapel in Tay Street before here) quitting the increasingly insalubrious city centre for the setting sun. Bourgeois solidity appears to be the idiom. Interior massively arcaded with two bay transepts.

231–233 Perth Road, 1823, William Burn
Small plain classical houses, first of an uncompleted crescent. **1–5 Blackness Avenue**, 1868, James Maclaren, form Dundee's best tenements – bay windows, carvings, pilasters and heavy string-courses. The city boasts few of the florid three-dimensional

middle-class tenements so prominent in
Glasgow, preferring detached suburbia. Pro-rata
to its population, it has one of the most extensive
suburbs of individual and semi-detached houses
in Scotland. An Edwardian enthusiast compared
the Blackness district to a Garden City.

Blackness Library, 225 Perth Road, 1904,
Frank Thomson
One of two libraries designed for his father
from his London digs (see Coldside p.129) this
ponderous red sandstone civic monument with
its Renaissance detailing and Ionic columns
contains a fine elliptical staircase, and an oval
upper hall with marble Doric columns.
Sculpture by Albert Hodge.

Blackness Library

7 **Seymour Lodge**, 259 Perth Road, 1880,
C & L Ower
Formidable pile with huge fretted barge-
boarded gables and soaring roofs capped by
panelled chimneystacks. Once a St Trinian's for
ladies drawn from the best local families, this
Gothic fantasy represents the kind of High
Victorianism favoured by American horror
movies. Magnificent streetscape. The Owers
were responsible for 1885 houses in like
manner at the bottom of Hyndford and
Rockfield Streets. Perth Road continues with
sporadic riparian development (of the kind
hated by planners) of a mixture of Regency
villas, humble cottages, gradually colonised by
great houses and public buildings.

*House for James Gentle, Hyndford
Street, 1883, by C & L Ower*

Seymour Lodge

West Park Centre

West Park, 319 Perth Road, 1860,
James Maclaren
Italianate with Greek key motif. **West Park
Centre**, 1992, J F Stephen, is the University's
Conference Centre. Fan-shaped on a single
level, the Centre is distinguished by its crisp
curving brickwork, tall window and angular
roof structure.

Duncarse, 381 Perth Road, 1858,
Charles Wilson
Large plain house with Italianate detail, well
perched upon a plateau overlooking the firth.
Stupendous conservatory encloses the entire
porch. Duncarse was built for George
Armitstead, later Lord Armitstead, a Russian
merchant from Archangel who married a
Baxter. The Baxters duly organised his election
to Parliament despite the fact that his
command of English was limited. After all, he
was *one of us*. Armitstead is commemorated by
a series of annual lectures in Dundee.

Binrock, 456 Perth Road, David Neave
Conversion by Neave of an 18th-century house
into good Regency with projecting bay, fanlit
doorway and stable block: skilfully extended by
Mills & Shepherd. After sale in 1923, Patrick
Thoms designed four houses in its grounds, of
which Greywalls is most notable.

48 **Greywalls**, 452 Perth Road, 1929,
Patrick Thoms
Wonderfully anachronistic Arts & Crafts house
(constructed entirely of stone perhaps from the
demolition of the Vault for the Caird Hall) set
snug into the hillside like a low-lying Cumbrian

Greywalls

manor house. Stone chimneys, stone slates, mullioned casement windows. A clever plan: forked like a *Y*, the twin gables joined by a loggia with the balcony above (in both of which are hooks for suspending the architect's hammock). Largely Arts & Crafts within (leaded window panes chosen by his wife), excellent timberwork, ingle-nook in both drawing room and hall.

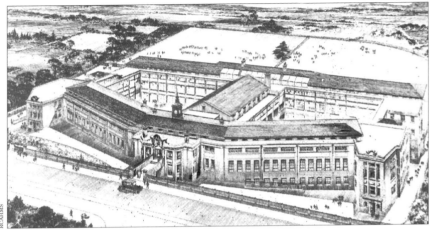

Harris Academy, 470 Perth Road, 1926–8, Donald Ross of Thoms & Wilkie Competition-winning design with plan of a large irregular courtyard split by hall. Single-storey appearance to the road, wings swept back from the formal stone entrance dominated by a cupola, and approached by drawbridge. Rear three-storey with largely glazed court façade. **Western Cemetery**, J R Findlater – an eye-blasting Gothic screen wall and gateway – so damaged by lightning as to resemble a decayed tooth.

Competition-winning drawing for the Harris Academy by Donald Ross

St Helen's, 474 Perth Road, 1850, Charles Wilson Vigorous neo-baronial banker's palace. Not a

Below left East façade of St Helen's. Below St Helen's as it is

Above *Tay Park*. Below *Hill Rise*
Right *Original elevation*

baronial purist, Wilson produced a mixed-media job: classical details, towers, crow-stepped gables and string-courses: i.e., one of Wilson's favoured Italianate palazzi picturesquely kitted out in a kilt. **Tay Park**, 484 Perth Road, is even freer – columned and pedimented porch with dormer windows above sandwiched between an overscaled turret and a crow-stepped gable. Wing, 1916, by Thoms & Wilkie.

49 **Ballochmyle**, 3 Norwood Crescent, 1880, J Murray Robertson
His own little house, and a miniature synthesis of what can be seen at much grander scale in the great villas of Broughty Ferry. Dominated by his leitmotif of the flattened stone tower with an ogee roof. **The Boreen**, 6 Westgrove Avenue, 1901, Thoms & Wilkie, is gracious Cumbrian rather than Scots, rubble with dressed stone quoins and projecting bays: the closest Thoms & Wilkie designed for other people to Patrick Thoms' Greywalls. Strong

similarity in the semicircular bays. **Hill Rise**, 21 Farington Street, 1914, Thoms & Wilkie, is sub-Lutyens, with its huge roof, tall chimney stacks and rubble walls.

Inniscarra, 385 Perth Road, 1905, William Williamson, utterly engaging, with its shaped Cape Dutch gables, sweeping red roofs, tall chimney stacks, balcony and ball-finialed bay windows. Nearby **Ardshiel**, 389 Perth Road, c.1905, by Thoms & Wilkie, is a delightful Arts

Above *Inniscarra*. Right *Ardshiel*

& Crafts cottage – part-harl, part-rubble, with a studiously asymmetrical façade.

Morar, 2 Hazel Avenue, *c*.1905, by Thoms & Wilkie, is prettily harled with projecting porch, oriel, turret, two-storey bay and leaded windows. **Narracoorte**, Hazel Avenue, 1952, by Gauldie Hardie Wright & Needham, has its principal rooms on the first floor, a fine double-height stair window, open planning typical of the period; early use of under-floor heating.

50 **Arnhall Gardens**, 1936, Lowe & Barrie
One of only two good 1930's houses in Dundee: white walls, flat roof, corner windows, cutaway corner for a balcony, and projecting semicircular bay to the drawing room. A small, fairly cheap house: making you wonder what might have been achieved had the money spent on some of the grander piles at this time been as adventurous architecturally. **5 Arnhall Drive**, *c*.1935, W W Friskin, is a plain cubic house enlivened by roundel, a sense of horizontality, and wrought-iron and tubular-

Top *Hall fireplace, 367 Perth Road.* Middle *Morar.* Above *Narracoorte.* Top left *Hazelhall (demolished) by Charles Wilson*

Left *Arnhall Gardens.* Below *East elevation*

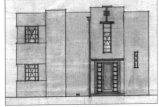

Nyoora

steel railings. Friskin's work in Dundee has been under-appreciated – particularly his churches and schools. The crafted brick of his 1938 chapel in Graham Street is an appropriate memorial.

West Dene, 504 Perth Road, 1903, Watson & Salmond, is largely Tudor – impact spoiled by replacing mullions with picture windows.

51 **Nyoora**, 514 Perth Road, 1905, Thoms & Wilkie, an elaborate red sandstone jute mansion in Scots Renaissance is, despite crafted stone and interior plasterwork, just too hard-edged to be credibly ancient. (colour page 72)

52 **Ardvreck**, 516 Perth Road, 1907, Mills & Shepherd
Sloping roofs, beautiful stone, mullioned windows, and gigantic asymmetrical circular arch unfolding the garden door. One of the finest Arts & Crafts houses in Scotland.

Ardvreck drawn by David Walker

Visitors' Centre

53 **Visitors' Centre**, University Botanic Gardens, Burnaby Street, 1982, Jack Fulton (colour page 72)
The Botanic Garden, established in 1971, is a delight, basking in its own microclimate and joyous setting on its sunny south-facing slope. The focus – at the end of the greenhouses – is this award-winning Visitors' Centre whose oversailing roof embraces the path. White concrete, black timber and transparent glass with strong geometric shapes represents Scottish modernism at its best. Within its tiny interior, a procession through different volumes and spaces. Used principally for exhibition and interpretation. **Vernonholme**, downhill, 1910, by David Baxter, swaddles Health

Board offices in Italianate classical, distinguished by a three-bay double-columned loggia.

The upper parts of Blackness formed the demesne of two estates – **Blackness House**, long, picturesque 17th-century mansion demolished before the Second World War, and **Balgay House**, once the seat of Morgan (of Morgan Academy). Balgay Hill and Victoria Park were acquired by the Corporation in 1870 as public parks, and offer sumptuous parkland, shrubbery and – particularly – views west up the Tay. The **Mills Observatory** was added in 1935.

Above *Blackness Manor House (demolished).* Left *Balgay House*

54 **Royal Victoria Hospital**, J Murray Robertson
The transformation of Balgay House, *c.*1760 – a pleasantly proportioned douce laird's mansion with pedimented door – into the core of an extensive hospital. Scots 17th-century in style derivative of Panmure House. The jagged
55 tower on the skyline below is that of **Parkview School**, Blackness Road, 1896, James Maclaren & Son: a tall H-plan French château with Dutch gables on the wings. **16 Kelso Street**, 1930s, comprises a pair of semi-detached *moderne* houses with metal-framed horizontally proportioned curving bay windows. **365 Blackness Road**, 1924, W Gauldie, is a small house with Arts & Crafts details in the stonework, and well-sculpted

The Blackness manor house depicted by Pont was a substantial and elaborate affair. What survived into contemporary history was a long graceful house, principal storey and attic sitting above a floor of cellars and kitchens, with a projecting round stair-tower. It thus formed part of a group with Murroes, Pitkerro, Gagie, Tealing, Wester Powrie and possibly Invergowrie. As compared to the vertically proportioned châteaux further north, with their elaborate skylines, this group of Renaissance country houses was a storey lower, more horizontal in emphasis, and less flamboyantly militaristic in profile than the bombastic Aberdonians.

Left *365 Blackness Road.*
Below *Parkview School*

Top *Mystery House*. Above *Duncraig*

chimney, focused upon a two-storey octagonal toplit hall.

56 **Mystery House**, corner of Blackness Road & Glamis Road, 1919
Largely unexceptional, vaguely L-plan, with balcony and curious history. In 1919, the City Architect James Thomson proposed to the Council that it should invest in a prototype house to test new materials, methods and services for the proposed Council housing estate in Logie. It was some time before a Councillor enquired what had happened. This was the house that Thomson had built (little like Logie), and the occupant was the City Architect himself. A walk down **Glamis Road** offers a nostalgic experience of tantalising glimpses of large houses of varying dates well concealed by high walls and luxuriant foliage: notably the overscale Franco-baronial **Duncraig**, 1890, by C & L Ower, roofscape details plundered from Morgan Academy (see p.129).

57 **Ninewells Hospital**, completed 1973, Robert Matthew Johnson-Marshall & Partners
One of the most distinguished 20th-century monuments in Dundee, if not Scotland. A medical campus dug into a sloping site to allow different levels of service access beneath the building. Being on the crest of the hill, the design could not be subsumed within a luxurious landscape like the same architects' Stirling University (see *Stirling & The Trossachs* in this series); instead it masses towards a focal point to provide sculptural form for the skyline. The tall, expressively tubular tower contains stairs and lift shafts beneath a

Cross-section through Ninewells Hospital & Medical School

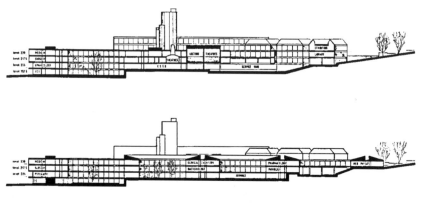

Left *Ninewells Hospital from the air.* Above *The concourse, not unlike an airport waiting room*

water tower. The plan – following the contemporary fashion of corridors as streets – radiates from the concourse, with double-height, cruciform columns, coffered ceiling, of the kind to be found at the better universities at the time. Plain façades of self-cleaning materials, generally two- and three-storey buildings are arranged around courtyards, (rather than the high-rise favoured at the time) central windows set back to provide balconies, and grid-like vents at eaves level. (colour page 72)

58 **Menzieshill**, 1963–5

Enormous development three miles north-west of the city centre on the northern slopes of Balgay Hill. Five, 15-storey blocks of flats containing overspilled inner city dwellers cleared by the *Trojan Ruins* from further in. Dundee never suffered from a loss of confidence, and Menzieshill – with its prominence – is as typical of its time as Reform Street, Victoria Road and Craigie. *The tall building artistically considered* was not a priority: package-deal blocks instead, with no named nor known architect.

Above *Clyde Place sheltered housing within Menzieshill, 1989, by DDC Architects. The western approaches:* Below *View west over Ninewells Hospital stair-tower up the Tay Valley into the heart of Perthshire.* Bottom *Looking the other way – a skyline of Menzieshill, with Ninewells Hospital on the right*

John Gray

Tay Works

Among the modern buildings in
*this place the spinning mills are not
to be overlooked – upon account of
their number, the multitude of
persons employed, the capital there
invested, and the profits which from
them have been derived. Till within
these last 30 years, the spinning of
yarns was effected by hand-wheels ...
but about or before that period,
attempts had been made to spin flax
by the means of machinery erected in
the mills. The attempts were found to
succeed so well, and to do the work so
much cheaper and better ... that the
number of mills has increased in this
town during the last 20 years ...
Aware of the demoralising tendency
of such great works, not a few of the
masters have introduced schools into
them.*
Second Statistical Account, 1833.

Bank of Scotland offices, West Port

Wishart

THE ROUTE NORTH WEST

The road to Coupar Angus rose also
immediately into rough rolling countryside: the
sort of place still a bit risky, in the early 19th
century, to stroll unaccompanied from Dundee
to Lochee. There was, first, the valley of the
Scouring Burn (now culverted, running
approximately the route of Guthrie Street to
Polepark); and then the Cox brothers'
extraordinary company town at Lochee. The
59 **West Port**, facing the exit from Overgate (now
marooned on the other side of the bypass),
forms a suitable gateway, marked by the island
block with its 1864 clock turret. The Scouring
Burn valley between Blackness Road and
Lochee Road became the Blackness Business
Development Area, and subject to urban
regeneration. How it has changed in 10 years!
Crumbly derelict mills have been converted to
flats, museums, workshops or warehouses;
gaps have been filled by factory units of brick
and curved wriggly metal roofs; and the Public
Arts Programme displays style and confidence.
Although Blackness still feels somewhat empty,
its monuments isolated, it is more of an
opportunity than a problem.

60 **Westport Bar**, 22a Henderson's Wynd East,
1980, Alan Phillips
The idiosyncratic conversion of a small
industrial shed into a bar: its stylishly modern
interior as Da Vinci had but a short life,
recollected only in the cutaway ziggurat
corners, windows and topless classical columns.

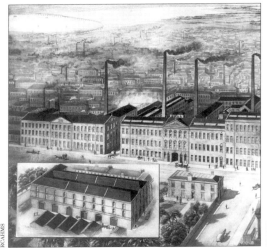

RCAHMS

RCAHMS

Tay Works, Lochee Road, 1851–65
Seat of the Gilroy brothers. Designed by their own engineers, this great industrial monument forms the entire western edge of Marketgait between Guthrie Street and Lochee Road. Having a massive, classical grim splendour, as befits possibly the largest textile mill in the United Kingdom (650ft long), it is ennobled by magnificent pediments with sculptures. Like most later Dundee mills, it is jack-arched for fireproofing reasons: iron roof trusses in its central loft are a superb example of Victorian engineering skill. The complex includes the 1830's Boyack Mill, the South Mill and the North Mill, begun 1851 by Joseph Lindsay. The façade was formerly capped by a statue of *Minerva*. Converted to **student residences**, with shops below, by Covell Matthews. The Gilroys were a manufacturing dynasty second only to the Baxters and the Coxs. Their ambition extended to owning plantations in India and their own jute freighters. Tay Works had to be as imposing as Dens, Camperdown or Bowbridge. (colour page 105)

South Mills, Brown Street, from 1825
The 14-bay Old Mill is the second oldest in Dundee; the 1851 New Mill is the third largest multi-storey mill in Dundee with an extraordinary Gothic attic structure upon rows of clustered columns. Built for J & W Brown, South Mills always spun flax.

Verdant Works, 27 West Henderson's Wynd, from 1833 (colour page 105)
Courtyard mill rebuilt much in 1852 after a fire.

Left *The Gilroy Empire: Tay Works and Blackness*. Above *Interior, Tay Works*

The Blackness Public Art programme, launched in 1982 as part of the regeneration of Blackness into a Business Development Area, includes award-winning ceramic panels by Keith Donnelly which fill window embrasures in Bellfield Street; the mural decorating the gable in St Peter's Street by Artists Collective depicting Dundee life; and a splendid mural by Stanley Bonnar symbolising the Indoor Bowls Club on Mylne Street. (colour page 105)

Between Lochee Road and Hawkhill clustered the greatest single concentration of mills and industrial buildings in Dundee. It swiftly became infamous: *there is probably not a more unsightly part of the town* said an 1873 **Guide** *from the combination of closely packed mills, and miserable unwholesome dwellings than that which stretches to the south of this once delightful Pleasance*. In 1912, the City's Housing Convenor expressed concern how the squalid conditions of the medieval *rookeries* had been *emulated by the modern crowded tenement, elbowed by the mill and jostled by the factory relieved from which the worker vanished into an adjacent close or pend*. By developing Craigie according to a Garden City layout, *along the happier ideas of our time*, he intended that *such districts as that lying between Lochee and Hawkhill can never be repeated*.

Verdant Works

Fine cast-iron Gothic roof, notable 1890 offices, 1833 building used as clocking-in lodge. Being converted by Stewart Tod & Partners to a Textile Heritage Centre for the Dundee Industrial Heritage Trust. West Henderson Wynd is stuffed with mills: the 1865 South Anchor Mill – jute weaving factory; the 1846 iron-framed and columned South Anchor Mill (now a stationery warehouse); the 1875 North Dudhope jute mill, and the 1834–6 Douglas jute mill.

St Mary Magdalene: Above *Exterior*. Right *Interior*

62 **St Mary Magdalene**, Blinshall Street, 1853–4, Coe & Goodwin
Secularised chapel-like church with bellcote, built as an Episcopal mission to the dark satanic mills of Blackness by Bishop Alexander Penrose Forbes. At one time the heart of the largest Episcopal congregation in Scotland, it had expensive Caen stone for dressings, a tiled reredos by William Butterfield, and stencilling which survives beneath the whitewash. *The Ecclesiologist* commented in 1855: *this very simple and cheap church appears to ask to be*

more richly deserving of praise for what it aims at, than the gorgeous and over-ladened palazzo with which the architect so accidentally won the first prize for the Foreign Office in the Italian style.

Logie Works, from 1828, Umpherston & Kerr
Founded by A & D Edward, Logie grew to be
Scotland's biggest flax works 1842–65. The
3 **Coffin Mill**, at the corner of Horsewater Wynd,
is properly the south range of the Logie Works.
It takes its name from a combination of its
coffin-shaped site, the true story of a fatal
accident during the construction of its chimney
tower, and the grisly legend of a mill lass whose
hair was caught in the machinery. Unusually
architectonic for a mill, with a seven-storey flat-
capped tower on the corner, and ranks of

The hospitality of the merchants to strangers is almost proverbial. As business is transacted now chiefly before dinner, the evening is devoted to domestic enjoyment, to useful introduction, to social parties or to the Club.
Second Statistical Account, 1833

Logie Works: Engine house windows

Left *Coffin Mill.* Below *Door to 24 Milnbank Road*

tripartite classical windows ennobling the
engine house. The **Edward Street Mill**, 1851,
part of the Logie Works, now the oldest
complete power loom factory in the city, is fully
iron-framed, with an unusually elaborate
interior to the engine house.

24 Milnbank Road, *c.*1815, David Neave
One of a pair of villas flanking Forrest Bank
Road, Ionic pilasters framing a doorway with a
fanlight and pediment above.

Harris Academy Annexe (formerly Logie
School), 1928, C G Soutar
A significant change from the Edwardian
School Board schools: horizontal, spreading

LOGIE

and surprisingly light in this formerly dark area. Largely glazed octagon, split by the school hall into two courtyards, harled with octagonal projecting stone bays, capped by pagoda and clock tower.

64 **College of Commerce Annexe** (former St Joseph's School), 126 Blackness Road, 1905–6, J H Langlands
A good comparison with Logie. Vertically proportioned, its designer was probably Langlands' associate W G Lamond (1854–1912) – his hand clearly identifiable in the turn-of-the-century details, and the large arched windows to double volume classrooms. Stylish eastern addition, 1933, by W W Friskin.

65 **St Joseph's Church**, Wilkie's Lane, 1874, Ellis & Wilson
Plain Gothic barn high on a hillock overlooking the city, with atmospheric interior (should it ever be unlocked). Huge 1900 reredos by Pugin & Pugin.

Logie Estate, 1919–20, James Thomson
The first municipal housing to be built in Scotland after the First World War, laid out in deliberate contrast to the rigidity of pre-war tenements. **Logie Avenue** is a short boulevard running to and from nowhere, intended originally to grow into *a majestic thoroughfare ... a thing of beauty and joy*. Unspectacular houses were designed to be a backdrop to greenery: greenery never burgeoned as intended, and the houses would benefit from whitewash. The layout is curvilinear for picturesque reasons as well as steepness, and the street names are determinedly rustic – **Ashbank Road**, **Lime Street**, **Elm Street**, and **Sycamore Place**. The estate was one of the first in Europe to have a district heating scheme, and pavements steamed in cold weather like New York (no longer: each house has its own central heating); and perhaps the first Scots municipal housing estate to be declared a Conservation Area. At the corner of **Balgay Road**, a block of brown brick flats, 1972, James Parr & Partners, terminates the row of tenements like a book-end.

66 Rising steeply from **City Road**, the small community around **Pitfour/Cleghorn Streets**, 1860s, resembles contemporary Colonies developments in Edinburgh – rows of douce, well-scaled two-storey terraced houses

Top *Harris Academy Annexe*. Middle *College of Commerce Annexe*. Above *Logie House (demolished), in the idiosyncratic classicism of James Black*

102

with gardens front and back: in reality, upper and lower flats entered from different sides of the building.

7 **St Francis Friary**, Tullideph Road, 1933, Reginald Fairlie
A real smack in the eye, crouching on its site as though embarrassed by its red brick – as alien to Dundee as a spaceship, until W W Friskin got going. Most of the money was spent on the monastery, so that the towering chapel planned by Fairlie had to be redesigned and built on a much smaller scale by A R Conlon, 1958, enhanced by the addition of a carved tympanum by Hew Lorimer.

THOU DIDST SIGN THY SERVANT FRANCIS O LORD WITH THE MARKS OF OUR REDEMPTIO

Top *Cleghorn Street cottages.*
St Francis Friary: Above *Tympanum by Hew Lorimer.* Left *Original design (uncompleted)*

Ancrum Road Primary School

Ancrum Road Primary School,
45 Ancrum Road, 1905, J H Langlands
Remodelling of an earlier school, and the first building for which W G Lamond had responsibility. His spoor may be spotted in the two-storey arcaded hall in the middle, the projecting staircases with climbing windows, lettering and the wavy parapet.

Above *Sheltered housing, Lochee Road by James Stephen.*
Right *Lochee Burns Club*

Bottom right *The over-clad Dudhope Court (DDC Architects, 1992), urban art in the foreground (colour page 106). Etched into the concrete tusks are commemorations of Dundonian celebrities including Mary Slessor (below) and Oor Wullie (bottom)*

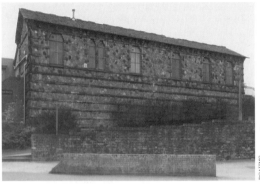

Lochee Burns Club (former station), 1860–1, James Gowans
Eye-catching north-facing stone wall with tall framed windows. Gowans was a master of masonry (and a substantial quarry-master) and a pioneer of modular design: everything was in multiples of 2ft. Like his other station at Creetown, Wigtownshire, this station displays a tempting array of varied reddish stones beneath its grime, panelled in Gowans' typical mode (see *Edinburgh* in this series).

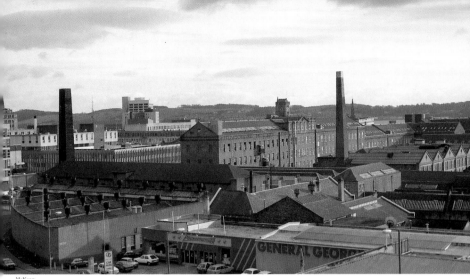

McKean

Dundee Museums & Art Galleries

Wishart

RCAHMS

Wishart

Wishart

Top *Tay Works & the Dundee skyline today*. Middle above
*Dundee in the early 19th century from above Lochee Road
painted by CGL Phillips*. Above *Offices of the Verdant Works*.
Right *Public art in Blackness*: above *'The Bridge' in
Hawkhill*; middle & below *Ceramic panels from a series by
Keith Donnelly, Bellfield Street.*

105

Above *Interior of St Salvador's*. Top left *Dudhope Castle*. Middle *Concrete houses in Court Street*. Left *Re-clad Dudhope Court*

Top *Morgan Academy*. Left *An idyllic (almost unreal) view of the Camperdown Works. St Ninian's Church to the left, jute palaces in their plantations lining the road to the left. Note particularly Cox's Stack and the private railway siding*. Above *Elevation of the western pavilion of Morgan Academy*

John Gray

RCAHMS

RCAHMS

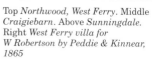

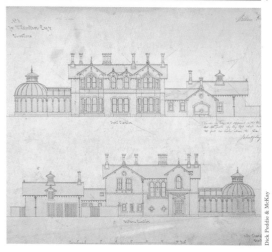

Dick Peddie & McKay

Top *Northwood, West Ferry*. Middle
Craigiebarn. Above *Sunningdale*.
Right *West Ferry villa for
W Robertson by Peddie & Kinnear,
1865*

Synagogue, St Mary's Place, 1987, Ian Imlach

Planet Bar, South Road, Lochee: 'architecture parlante'

Left *Lochee High Street, c.1860.* Below *Cox's Stack*

LOCHEE

Lochee owed its existence to the Lochee Burn which powered its mills, and to Dundee which acted as the market. Virtually a company town, its origins date to the arrival of a manufacturer called Cock (from a bleaching family) in Locheye *c.*1700. By 1777, David Cock had 280 hand-looms at work. Known after 1851 as Cox Brothers, his descendants pioneered manufacture of jute cloth. Their fiefdom was the 35-acre **Camperdown Works** and 5000 retainers. Between 1841–51, the population of Lochee quadrupled. After production ceased in 1981, Camperdown's ruins (after some tidying

LOCHEE

Camperdown Works at the height of its glory (colour page 107)

New Camperdown

up) starred in the BBC drama *Christabel*, representing war-torn Berlin in 1944.

Designed by George Cox (with kindly advice from Peter Carmichael of the Dens), the Camperdown Works were gargantuan in scale. Mostly single-storey sheds, the site was dominated by the giant **Sliver** or **High Mill**, 70ft tall, almost one-tenth of a mile long, with a 100ft tower with a cast-iron cupola at the east end: cathedral-like in grandeur – an imagery enhanced by its campanile, the lacy Gothic roof structure in its 40-bay attic like a surreal Gothic cloister. Prominent block of flats for Servite Housing Association by James F Stephen reflects the powerful scale of the High Mill, which is to be converted into flats. The **Calendar Building**, 1861–5, which later housed what was considered to be the largest calendaring (finishing) machine in Europe (now homeless), has been redeveloped within the screen walls as a supermarket, retaining only its front bays. The bleach and dyeworks and jute warehouses have been replaced by social and private housing: and the warehouses, 1861, by the former railway siding (Camperdown was the only jute works in Dundee to have its own branch railway) have also been converted into flats. (colour page 51)

The boiler-house arcade screen and the 280ft-high **Cox's Stack**, by James Maclaren & G A Cox, remain as features linking the housing to commercial development. The polychromatic brickwork of the Stack is weakly echoed in the walls of the large sheds camouflaging cinema, nightclub, bar, fish-and-chips restaurant, bingo hall, megabowl and amusement arcade enfolding an acreage of asphalted car-parking. The (former)

110

Half-Timer's School, Bright Street, 1884, probably James Maclaren, does time as a Boys' Brigade Hall.

Spire of St Ninian's

St Ninian's, Methven Street, 1829–30, David Neave
Symbolising the totality of Cox control of Lochee, the Parish Church lies at the works gate: a plain box kirk with two storeys of windows, shallow pilasters topped by a pediment, itself capped by a pleasant stone spire.

St Mary's Church, 41 High Street, 1865, J A Hansom
Exceptional building designed by the London architect who founded *The Builder* magazine and designed the original Hansom Cab.

St Mary's Church: Below *Exterior.* Left *Interior*

111

Transformed by the octagonal, buttressed and prismatically roofed chancel (which also does duty as a spire), the atmosphere within is mystical: polychromatic – grey stone, yellow brick and red sandstone, with superb detail and craftsmanship. The world outside is shut away by the heavily enclosing walls.

Library & Public Baths

Fortress-like Clydesdale Bank

Library & Public Baths, 1894–6,
J Murray Robertson
Lovely red stone building paid for by the Coxs, with Jacobean details, string-courses, panelling and gables – barrel-vaulted library within. *The Builder* considered it *one of the most satisfactory buildings we have noticed.* Recently refurbished by DDC Architects. **Church Hall**, Gray's Lane, 1934, W W Friskin, is brick *moderne,* not unlike a miniature cinema.

Clydesdale Bank, 93 High Street, 1876,
C & L Ower
Not in their American Gothic but equally rogue baronial – topped by vividly superfluous corbels. **Savings Bank**, 1903, David Baxter, typical neo-Renaissance which Baxter used for this series of banks throughout Dundee.
Lochee West Kirk, 191 High Street, James Maclaren, has a Gothic façade and spire.
Lochee Cabinet Factory, 127 South Road, 1911, was a brick and stone transformation of an 1860 power loom factory to a Caroline furniture works by Thoms & Wilkie.

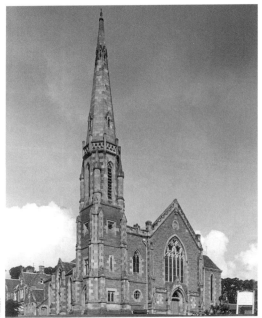

70 **Florence Booth House** (former Clement Park), Harefield Road, 1844, James Maclaren Last surviving jute palace in Dundee, built for James Cox, chief promoter of the Tay Railway Bridge (recollected with his wife Clementina in

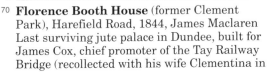

the stained glass monograms JC and CC). For Dundee, this mansion is unusually close to t'mill. A lavishly twin-towered stone confection from variously plundered styles ranging from thin medievalism to Caroline gables.

Beechwood, the Saltire Society award winner of 1938, is destined for demolition, rather than recapturing the original optimism implied by the brick and iron entrance details.

Dundee District Libraries

Dudhope Castle & Lochee Road, c.1803. The ruins of Broughty Castle are in the far distance: St Andrew's spire and the skyline half left. To the right can be seen the Trades Hall dome rising above the Howff, the Town House and – behind Corbiehill with its windmill – the Old Steeple

SECOND SUBURB:
Chapelshade & Dudhope

Chapelshade and Dudhope embrace the sunny south-facing slopes of the Law sandwiched between Lochee Road and Hilltown, north of the Inner Ring Road. Originally, Chapelshade was a small higgledy suburb just to the north of Albert Square (now much beneath the ring road) clustering around a **Chapel of Ease**. It was criticised in 1824 for *the same irregularity of plan and building which seems endemic amongst those of the inhabitants who have it in their power to make themselves comfortable, if only they could bear to communicate some portion of the same to their neighbours*. In 1833, David Mackenzie brought it style in the form of two steep horseshoe streets further up the slope, above the then smoke level. But Dundee expanded too rapidly and, like other early suburbs in Hawkhill, Milnbank and Arbroath Road, Chapelshade was swiftly overwhelmed by factories and foundries.

71 **Dudhope Castle**, from 1580 (colour page 106) *A noble and ancient pile* (as Defoe put it) dramatically set on a bluff overlooking the city, principal seat of the Scrymseours (or Scrymgeours), hereditary Constables of Dundee, from whom it passed to Lord Hatton and then Bonnie Dundee – John Graham of Claverhouse. What you now see are two wings of a 16th/17th-century palace enfolding a courtyard, the tower depicted by Slezer demolished. Conical roofed towers mark each corner and flank the pended entrance capped by a dumpy bellcote astride a corbelled

Dudhope Castle

pediment added by Samuel Bell in 1790. The 1989 works by DDC Architects (A B Anderson) restored harling, conical roofs to the entrance towers and the corbelled stair-tower rising from the first floor of the north façade (but not its once-prominent dormer windows). This was a place of magnificence – symbolised, not least, by the fact that Charles Maitland, Lord Hatton, brother of the Duke of Lauderdale,

Left *The newel stair in Dudhope Castle.* Below *Dundee College of Commerce, Constitution Road*

The Royal Infirmary earned the following perceptive critique from Patrick Allan–Fraser, the artist who remodelled Hospitalfield, near Arbroath (Sir Walter Scott's Monkbarns) in 1854: *It is merely an imitation of an English baronial residence consistent with its exterior form. This building, besides two long octagonal towers in front and the usual profusion of gables common to the style, has two large pretentious towers one on each of the two sides of the main building. Now in really old Elizabethan houses, towers were not erected for ornament merely, but were considered necessary additions to the internal accommodation ... Those two towers standing so prominent and claiming to be considered principal features are really of no service in respect of their not affording any additional useful accommodation. They are four storeys in height. The first three merely serve to prolong the passages beyond where any passage is required, and the fourth storey, although apparently intended to serve some useful purpose, is not furnished with doors or any openings by which they could be entered.*

The Royal Infirmary
Built to replace the original in King Street (immediately transformed to model lodgings and now demolished), the Royal Infirmary was the first building to separate medical, surgical and fever wards. The £14,000 raised (largely by subscription) proved to be inadequate: the building was the cause of a claim for additional payments by the builder. In February 1855 the *Building Chronicle* reported, with some glee, that *now that the building is finished the Directors are at a loss what to do with it, the unusually healthy condition of the town and the enormously expensive accommodation of the new buildings being rather striking. It is accordingly being offered to the government as a hospital for sick and wounded soldiers.*

ennobled it with new interiors when his brother was doing the same at Thirlestane. It declined to a woollen mill and then – with a new floor inserted – to a barracks and to a storehouse. Now in better condition than at any time since the mid-18th century, Dudhope is let as high-class offices.

Valentine & Son

72 **Dundee Royal Infirmary**, Barrack Road, 1853–5, Coe & Goodwin (*above*)
Elizabethan pile with a central gatehouse with a corbelled oriel window of an Oxbridge College sort, functionally useless octagonal towers terminating each wing. Scotland's fascination with towers is satisfied by the central one above the gatehouse terminating in a cupola.
Garland Place, 2–10 Barrack Road, 1867, and **Rustic Place**, 1–5 Dudhope Street, 1870–5, are unusually high-quality tenements by William Alexander, with neo-Tudor details and rare corbelled balconies, turning the Constitution Road corner.

RCAHMS

73 **St Mary Magdalen Episcopal**, 1867, Edward & Robertson (*above*)
Tall, Gothic, buttressed (if badly skinned) Catholic Apostolic Church with a flèche. As normal with the Catholic Apostolic, it is the interior that matters – stencilled roof, notable stained glass, rich fittings – all as appropriate

for a church which sought to immerse its celebrants in ritual.

2–4 Constitution Terrace, 1851, James Maclaren

4 **Prospect Place** and **Laurelbank** form David Mackenzie's two steep, cramped horseshoes of Constitution and Union Terraces. These lovely houses are Dundee's riposte to Blacket Place, Edinburgh: an enclave of villas and semi-detached villas with a variety of picturesque details such as Dutch gables, finials, Greek key balconies, decorative garden walls and mature bushes. **2–4**, semi-detached U-plan, framed by projecting curvilinear gables, are delicate Jacobean, decorated with hood-moulds, curvilinear dormers and tall slender chimneys. **16**, 9 years later, is similarly picturesque but more elaborate – with crenellations, strapwork and niches. **1–4 Somerville Place**, 1830, James Black, is a tiny development of semi-detached harled Regency villas with stone margins, with fanlit doorways so remote from their parent as to seem detached. **4** has fine plaster and timberwork.

5 **1–5 Dudhope Terrace**, 1840, George Angus
A rank of self important, albeit small, neoclassical villas with massive Doric porches. These form part of Angus's plan of exploiting the wonderful slopes of the Law with classical cottages and villas. Smaller variants, more delicate, are **1–2 Panmure Terrace**.

Dudhope House, 1850, Charles Wilson
Engorgement of a classical predecessor in Scots 17th-century – corbels, crow-steps, gunloops and parapet strapwork: a fashion plate of what the *Building Chronicle* criticised as baronial perversity five years later: *Now in North Britain we have old Scottish – thanks to Burn*

The dying letter of **William Knight**, a local poet, was written from the Infirmary in 1866: *I was in comfortable lodgings, but the fever broke over Dundee like an avalanche … My lodging-house folks were attacked almost simultaneously. My landlady was carried to the Royal Infirmary: next, her eldest boy. Next, the landlord himself was seized … But now my turn came … I had no pain and was getting as much as 12oz of unreduced whisky every 24 hours, so that I was always half-seas over …*

Left *Constitution Terrace*. Below *Prospect Place*. Bottom *Dudhope Terrace*

117

and Billings' Baronial Antiquities – taking its place, as, par excellence, the style of nine-tenths of our domestic buildings; and oh! what oddities are being perpetrated in its name. The grim bastion towers of Caerlaverock and Craigmillar are being revived in the retreats of peaceable country gentlemen; heavy battlements surmount their doorway and loopholes command it.

76 **8–12 Dudhope Street**, 1850, David Mackenzie
Architectural minestrone: Doric-columned porches, ball finials and yet (**10**) surmounted by crow-steps. Further terraces are cut into the Law ranging from simple Victorian cottages facing unmade roads (**Adelaide Place**) to the more substantial mansions downhill, like the Italianate **10–11 Albany Terrace**, 1877, Young & Meldrum, and **3 Douglas Terrace**, 1882, by William Alexander, both with Italianate windows, quoins, campanile, etc.

Below *8 Panmure Terrace*.
Right *10–11 Albany Terrace*

McKean

RCAHMS

Druimbeg

RCAHMS

77 **8 Panmure Terrace**, 1872,
Frederick T Pilkington
The manse for the McCheyne Memorial Church (see p.88). Pilkington achieves something unusually delicate in the proportions of this simple two-storey villa with its projecting bay window, and its polychromatic banding. The upper storey of the bay seems almost entirely glass – rather like a Gothic Alexander Thomson. **Druimbeg**, 3 Panmure Terrace, 1909, James Tough, has the turn-of-the-century details that one would expect, knowing that Lamond was assisting him as a *homer*. The details of **2 Panmure Terrace** recall those of the Vine.

High Church, Kinghorn Road, 1879,
Ireland & Maclaren
Forms a roughly detailed Gothic landmark on
the skyline when seen from the Tay. **War
Memorial**, 1921, Thomas Braddock, won in a
competition assessed by Sir Robert Lorimer.

Above *Cottage in Lawside Road by
and for Thoms & Wilkie.* Left *St
Joseph's Convent*

St Joseph's Convent of Mercy, Gardner
Street, Lawside, 1892, Archibald MacPherson
Of all the Gothic buildings in Dundee this
higher grade of school for 60 young ladies most
conveys authenticity by its soaring gables,
austere massing, tall but thin proportions and
quality details.

HILLTOWN & THE NORTH
Hilltown clustered around the ancient north
route from Dundee as it rose up the steep
incline from the Ladywell. Lying beyond the
burgh's regality and mercantile restrictions, it
was encouraged by the Constables of Dundee to
manufacture goods in rivalry, but, being
outside the walls, was likely to be sacked by
any army commander – such as the Marquess
of Montrose – who wanted to avoid taking on
the entire town. The building pattern was one
of street frontages with long riggs behind, later
developed into courts, wynds and alleys, and
populated by craft trades remembered in
Bonnet Hill and **Bucklemaker Wynd**. After
the cutting of **King Street**, and the
construction of **Victoria Road** through
Bucklemaker Wynd provided a gentler ascent

War Memorial on Dundee Law

119

to Forfar, Hilltown was bypassed, its cottages speedily engulfed with factories, worthy churches and serried ranks of very plain tenements.

78 **18–20 Victoria Road**, 1877, Pilkington & Bell
Extravagant corner block whose attic storey runs to a different rhythm than the rest, acting as clerestory (Thomson again) punctuated by encrusted Italianate corbels which prop up the roof. In **Forebank** some late 18th-century suburban houses remain to be discovered.

Top *Hilltown clock, 1911.*
Above *Cobbler's shop window,*
Strathmartine Road. Top right
Dundee Pie Shop, Hilltown. Right
18–20 Victoria Road

Wishart

Wishart

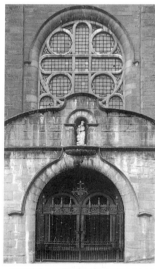

Wishart

RIAS Collection

'9 **St Mary's Forebank**, Powrie Place, from 1850, George Mathewson
The interior of Mathewson's huge barn is pretty powerful anyway – immensely rich, barrel-vaulted, Romanesque, whose muscular round-headed arches march towards the altar. The exterior was transformed, 1900, by W G Lamond, T M Cappon's assistant, who added the twin campaniles tied by the screen wall at ground level, combining echoes of hillside Tuscany with the most advanced art nouveau, providing the city with its most uplifting skyline. **School** added by Ireland & Maclaren. Immediately above, **Powrie Place**, 1981, DDC

Wishart

St Mary's Forebank: Top *The campaniles from Powrie Place.* Middle *The principal entrance.* Above *Detail: note the sinuous stonework.* Top left *The eastern façade.* Left *Interior*

121

2 Kinghorn Road

In 1756 only one Hilltown house had a slate roof, the remainder being thatched. The *bonnet makers had all seats at the end of their houses where they sat and wrought their bonnets with large wires. The houses in general had the gables to the streets, but were only a ground floor covered with thatch, but many only with divots of earth ... only a few of them had glass windows.* By 1834, the district consisted of *irregular ill-built houses, but interspersed with many manufactories where cloths are prepared, chiefly for the merchants and agents in the Wellgate and Murraygate, who send them abroad to the remotest corners of Asia and America.*

St Salvador's Church

Hilltown underwent a second redevelopment as tenements in the late 19th century. In 1912, the then City's Housing Convenor condemned how they ran *in straight rows against the skyline, practically sunless in the ground flats compelling the children to play, and the wayfarer to pass as if between two tall, draught creating and sun obstructing stone dykes, almost completely blocking out the fine views ... Notoriously it presents all the conditions favourable to consumption ... We can see the process of slum creation proceeding under our very eyes.*

Architects (R Brunton), has low, sweeping, slate roofs so as not to obscure the view of those towers.

Windmill Bar, Hilltown
18th-century survival incorporated into an 1868 stepped tenement block with grotesque human and animal masks in the window surrounds (similar to the tenement in North Ellen Street by John Bruce, and for the same client). **2 Kinghorn Road**, 1934, William Patrick, has a flashy shopfront with black vitrolite, metal strips, diamond-paned glass, and horizontally proportioned windows.

Hilltown West, 1973, Bett Brothers, further developed 1980–1 by DDC Architects (G Birrell & C Wishart), provides variegated roofscape, good landscaping and colourful material – representative of Dundee's romance with vernacular cottages for city centre living. A more coherent urban approach is now preferred. Dominant visual feature is the four 23-storey blocks of flats in **Maxwelltown**, 1965–8, Ian Burke, Martin & Partners.

80 **St Salvador's Church**, St Salvador's Street, 1865–75, G F Bodley (colour page 106) Another city mission built for the ecclesiological Bishop Alexander Penrose Forbes, with sufficient internal vividness and luxuriance to promote immediate conversion. Bodley once compared his churches to a jewel casket, and so it is here. Within this simple rose-windowed hall you are in a world of turquoise and green, sumptuously rich stencilled wall decoration, open roof, reds and yellows. Restoration begun in 1972 by R Snowden under Colin McWilliam, and continued under Simpson & Brown. The **Caldrum Works**, St Salvador's Street, 1872,

Robertson & Orchar, was the first really large (six mills, six sheds) textile mill in the United Kingdom to integrate spinning, weaving and finishing in a single production unit.

Servite House, Alexander Street, 1987, J F Stephen
Crisp L-shaped block of 44 dwellings for local elderly people, notable for the way it rises to the scale of adjacent tenements. Turns the recessed corner with a billowing ground-floor glazed common room, courtyard behind with dinky red-painted gable. Otherwise, sharp detail, articulated windows and sufficient relief for sunshine to create patterns.

Manhattan Works, 1874, Thomson Brothers
Single-storey jute spinning mill for Colonel Sandeman, the courtyard dominated by a horizontal entrance house, re-fronted by Findlay & Smith, 1908.

Top St Mary's flats, Mains Road, 1936. Above Servite House

Court Street, 1875, David Clunas
Innovatory mass concrete houses by architect responsible for the new working men's tenements in Blackfriars Street, Edinburgh, possibly carrying out experiments impossible in the Capital (Dundee was quite interested in concrete). Built for the Working Men's Housing Association (Clunas' Edinburgh client was also an artisans' co-operative) by the Concrete Building Company, the houses have good proportions, cornices and mouldings. Renovation in 1984 by DDC Architects revealed that quality control during original construction was similar to that of the first Tay Bridge.

The Connies – the concrete houses of Court Street (colour page 106)

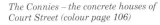

123

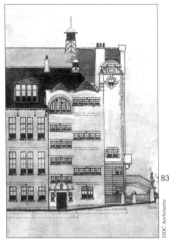

Morgan Academy Annexe: Top right
Central well. Top *Detail of the 1906
drawing*. Above *Exterior*

SS Peter & Paul Church

83 **Morgan Academy Annexe** (former Stobswell
School), Eliza Street, 1906, W G Lamond
Built under the auspices of J H Langlands,
School Board Architect, as the mixed-sex
Stobswell Supplementary showpiece school for
children over 14 (later restricted to girls). One
of Scotland's most important Edwardian
buildings, comparable to Mackintosh's Scotland
Street school in Glasgow. The design is
generated by a double-height arcaded central
hall creating a galleried space with diffused
light. The school pioneered teaching of
technical and domestic science with art and
cookery rooms, physics lab, metal workshop
and a housewifery department (a complete
miniature Edwardian teaching house). Art
nouveau details everywhere – in case fittings,
balconies, exposed roof trusses, external
lettering, wavy parapet and central heating
duct. **Clepington School**, Sandeman Street,
1892, was designed by J H Langlands before he
took on Lamond as assistant: comparable in
scale and grandeur, it lacks the unique flavour.

SS Peter & Paul RC School, 1930,
W W Friskin
Unpretentious long two-storey wings, whose
attractive entrance has Byzantine details and
good wrought iron, in homage to the 1928
84 **SS Peter & Paul Church**, Reginald Fairlie,
alongside: reticent gable to a red brick barn (by
contrast Jack Coia's near contemporary St
Anne's, Whitevale Street, Dennistoun, focuses
all upon a façade unrelated to what lies
behind); red brick walls within offset by white
octagonal columns and mystical apse. Fairlie
was a master of atmospheric interiors.
Rockwell Central School, Lawton Road,
1929–30, W W Friskin, is probably his
friendliest – purple brick with red brick details.

Top *The Knapp Mill painted 1950 by J McIntosh Patrick (by courtesy of Dr Jacob).* Above *General Accident Data Processing Centre, Technology Park.* Top right *Grianan Building, Dundee Technology Park.* Middle *Original drawing of Grayburn.* Right *Inside St Marnoch's, Fowlis Easter*

Top right *Mains Castle*. Right
Dunbar Park. Top *Entrance hall to
the new factories at Claverhouse,
DDC Architects, 1993*. Above
Dundee / Newtyle railway line

Wishart

Dundee Museums & Art Galleries

Wishart

RIAS Collection

Top *Camperdown House.* Middle
*Billiard room fireplace, Camperdown
House.* Above *Low & Bonar offices.*
Left *Berry-picking, Mains of Gray,
painted, 1967, by J McIntosh Patrick*

127

John Gray

RCAHMS

Dundee Museums & Art Galleries

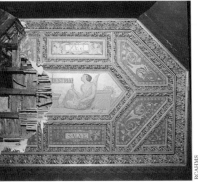

RCAHMS

Top *Interior of St Luke's, Broughty Ferry.* Above *Opening of the Dundee/Arbroath railway: the inaugural train as it passes the Royal Tay Yacht Club painted by George McGillivray.* Above left *Dining room ceiling from Carbet Castle.* Left *South entrance porch ceiling to Carbet Castle (demolished)*

Coldside Library, 130 Strathmartine Road, 1908, Frank Thomson
Thomson's most sophisticated library: concave-fronted Y-plan library, massive baroque gables facing Strathmore Avenue and Strathmartine Road. Transformed by a blind upper storey in sheer, bright red brick.

Coldside Library: Left *Original perspective*. Above *Main entrance*

Lawside Works
Spinning mill founded in 1830s, carpet weaving factory added by Robertson & Orchar in 1888, with an Italianate bellcote. Lit by electricity from the very beginning.

King's Cross Hospital, 1889
Octopus plan of detached wards for the treatment of infectious diseases. Excellent MacFarlane cast-iron railings. In the grounds by Clepington Road lies a wayside halt for the Dundee & Newtyle Railway, 1831.

371 Clepington Road, 1873, J & A Leslie
Sluice chamber for Dundee Water Commissioners: curious castellated confection that regulated water pressure. **The Clep**, 96–98 Clepington Road, 1941, James MacLellan Brown – rare war-time survivor: period-piece bar, scarcely altered within.

NORTH-EAST ROUTE TO FORFAR
In 1871, George Shaw Aitken won the competition for a gentler route to the north-east; not a trace of his development through Bucklemaker Wynd remains. **Victoria Road** has been transformed by losing its south side to the **Wellgate**, comprising houses, a shopping centre and a ring road. The houses, 1972–4, DDC Architects, represented a rejection of Dundee's urban past in favour of picturesque pantiled and coloured harling transplanted from Fife fishing villages. The landscape design includes *tot lots* for children under seven. East Neuk transplants are user-friendly: this one earned a Saltire Society Commendation and a Civic Trust Award.

Wellgate

Above *Trinity Church elevation.*
Right *A & S Henry's Calendar*

[87] A & S Henry's Calendar, 60 Victoria Road,
1874–5, Robertson & Orchar
A calendar was a finishing works: and this was
appropriately grand: made even more so when
converted to the headquarters of A & S Henry
with its opulent marble staircase and
boardroom panelling (stolen whilst derelict).
The façade is a two-dimensional rendering
from the Billings drawing in the *Building
Chronicle*. Conversion to 43 flats and office
space by Jack Fulton Associates.

(Former) **Trinity Church**, 72 Victoria Road,
1877, J G Fairley
Florid stuff: white stone, pinnacles, enormous
rose window – all in early French Gothic – until
you reach the ground floor where the entrance
is sandwiched between two shopfronts,
confirming Thomas Hood's 1815 satire:
*And their rooted dislike and aversion to waste
Is suffered sometimes to encroach on their taste;
For beneath a theatre or chapel they'll pop,
A saleroom or warehouse, or mean little shop.*

Provost James Guthrie Orchar
of Broughty Ferry and Provost
William Robertson of Dundee
designed, built and fitted machines
and buildings for jute works from
the Wallace Foundry. Both had
raised themselves from very humble
beginnings. They were responsible
for Bowbridge and Seafield Works,
and the Victoria Road Calendar.
Their in-house architect must have
been a creative man, for nine other
buildings may also have been
designed by them. When the
demand for such work slackened in
Dundee, they exported to America
and then to Calcutta. In doing so, it
is arguable that they sold to the
Indians the weapons the latter
needed to process jute themselves
independently of the West – thereby
pulling the bung from Dundee's
economy.

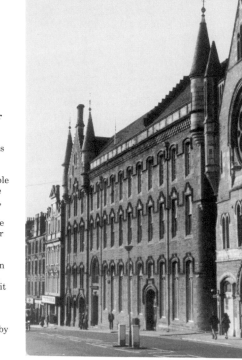

Adjacent **78–86 Victoria Road** tenements,
also by Fairley, continue the baronial theme.

Dens Road follows the line of the culverted
Dens Burn, which explains why it is lined with
mills which drew feedwater from it. They
included the **Eagle Mills**, 1864; the **Baxter
Brothers' Foundry** transformed to a new
spinning mill in 1930, with art deco pediment
by Robert Gibson; the **Wallace Works**, 25
Arthurstone Terrace, 1840 and 1853 – a
weaving and finishing building – east-end
entrance a little two-storey mansion with
quoins, aedicule and an arcaded ground floor;
the **Wallace Foundry** (which made
locomotives for the Dundee & Arbroath
Railway); the **Dura Works**, 1834–6, L-plan
iron-framed mill with tripartite engine house
windows; red sandstone **Blakey's Mill**,
1834–6, now converted to flats; and the
Rashiewell Works, 1855, has become the
Dens Road Market with scarcely any
alteration. Not even the magnificent gateway
surmounted by a camel (Grimond symbol)
survives of the **Bowbridge Works**, 1857,
extended in 1885 by Robertson & Orchar for
another of the principal Dundee dynasties –
the Grimonds. In its heyday, Bowbridge
employed over 3000 people offering *a
comfortable dining room, lavatories, and a
large hall for amusement and lectures.*

Below *Crescent Lane housing by
DDC Architects, mid 1980s.*
Middle *Arthurstone Library.*
Bottom *St Patrick's Church*

88 **Arthurstone Library**, Arthurstone Terrace,
1903, W Alexander
Completed by James Thomson, after
Alexander's death, Arthurstone was the first
branch library opened by Andrew Carnegie to
relieve pressure on the library in the Albert
Institute. Renaissance details and an elaborate
upstairs reading room. **Arthurstone Terrace**
was named after Peter Carmichael of the Dens,
who had bought the estate of Arthurstone in
Perthshire.

St Patrick's Church, 3 Arthurstone Terrace,
1897, T M Cappon
There was clearly money in this district when
St Patrick's was built in its red rubble, the
tower capped by an octagonal belfry. It is
thoroughgoing Scots revival – splendid window
tracery, Dunblane buttresses, and the vent in
the belfry modelled upon St Mary's oculus. The
sinuous curving parapets above the
confessionals reveal the hand of W G Lamond,

Dens Road School: Above *Principal elevation showing the characteristic stair-towers and ventilation.* Right *Principal corridor.* Below *Trinity Church Hall.* Bottom *Ogilvie Church.* Below right *Inside Ogilvie Church*

who had replaced Harry East as Cappon's assistant. In the **Dens Road School**, 1908, slightly further up, Lamond reveals himself as now having moved across to J H Langlands, the School Board Architect, in the prominent turn-of-the-century central heating intake and ventilators, curvy parapet and lettering.

Trinity Church Hall (former Savings Bank), 146 Princes Street, 1914, David Baxter's normal Edwardian Renaissance banker's mode, with an unorthodox domed clock tower. **Ogilvie Church**, 1876, Edward & Robertson, presents different faces to all winds at the gushet of Dura and Albert Streets. The slated Scots spire, lozenge-shaped when seen from the west is different when seen from the east.

Stobswell (former Park) **Church**, 18 Park Avenue, 1898–9, Leslie Ower, is rather better, its galleried, beautifully intimate interior imaginatively converted to flats above and doctors' surgery below by Architectus, 1993.

89 Morgan Place, 1930s,
James MacLellan Brown
Stone courtyard development of council houses,
with towers at the corners: austere, but good
housing within a genuine Scots character. In
Craigie Street, is a 1981 version by DDC
Architects, using blockwork and masonry and
lifts to create a group of contemporary Scots
tower houses. Its much brighter colours give a
good lead as to how Scottish townscape might
develop in the future.

Above *Craigie Street*. Left *Morgan
Academy from the air*

Wellfield Works, 1866
Jute-spinning mill with twin engine houses,
the height now useful for plastic packaging.

Founded by a returned nabob,
John Morgan, the **Morgan
Academy** was conceived as a
Dundonian George Heriot's Hospital
(Edinburgh) – for the education of
180 *sons of tradesmen and persons
of the working class generally whose
parents stand in need of assistance.*
Those who had entertained
expectations from Morgan
challenged his Will in the Court of
Session, compelling Dundee's Nine
Trades to fight to the House of Lords
on behalf of the Burgh's interest. By
the time they won, with the Will
proven, the substance had (as in
Jarndyce v Jarndyce in Dickens'
Bleak House) been so reduced as to
fund an initial foundation for only
60 boys. Since construction could not
begin until 1863, the original
designs could be continually varied.

90 Morgan Academy, 1850–68,
Peddie & Kinnear (colour page 107)
Set on a balustraded terrace on a high slope
overlooking Dundee, its stylistic similarity to
1862–70 Fettes College, Edinburgh, by David
Bryce, is quite striking, although the latter is
much later, larger, considerably more rigorous,
and in a much more elaborate parkland
setting. Two wings of classrooms branch from
the striking central turreted tower. Flanking
wings are embellished with Flemish gables and
elaborate carving to the windows, surmounted

The strict governing regulations
of the Morgan Academy required
that *the more degrading kinds of
corporal punishment shall be
avoided or resorted to as seldom as
possible, and never for mere literacy
deficiency if unaccompanied with
moral blame.*

1992 extension of Morgan Academy

133

by iron cresting on the roof. Were Fettes not available for comparison, one would revel even more in the exuberance of Morgan's turrets, chimneys, dormer windows, oriels and tracery. Two tall extensions pay obeisance: one by J H Langlands, 1914–1915, and a 1992 riposte by Tayside Region Architects. The ensemble suffers from the removal of its railings.

7–11 Madeira Street, 1870, Revd G A Harris Idiosyncratic Gothic cottages by an architect minister, presumably intended to empathise with the Academy. Harris also designed **3–11 Forfar Road** at the same time.

Dundee Waterworks, corner of Stobsmuir/Clepington Road, 1908 A castellated confection in muddy Dundee stone squatting above the 1848 reservoir, detailed by David Baxter to assist his brother George, the Water Engineer.

91 **53–55 Forfar Road**, 1905 Curious pair of red sandstone semi-detached bungalows designed by W G Lamond for his employer J H Langlands, deploying the Bangladesh idea of the bungalow as a single-storey house far beyond the traditional notion of cottage: splayed walls, battered chimney, horizontally proportioned Arts & Crafts corner bays capped by Indian roofs. **57** Forfar Road, 1905–10, Hutton & Tough, has mullion-windowed bays with a broad verandah between, a balcony above sheltered by broad eaves.

7-11 Madeira Street

53-55 Forfar Road

Albert Street
Albert Street is the last surviving main 19th-century arterial route into Dundee to retain its streetscape of working-class tenements, associated shops, etc. Those on the corner of **Arthurstone Terrace**, 1900, *really splendid specimens of the latest and most approved tenements and houses*, were erected as a model block of working men's dwelling houses. Crow-stepped, with string-courses delineating each floor, projecting bay windows capped by turrets, quoins and other rubbly details, they have a chunky grandeur that is as much part of Dundee's history as West Ferry.

Baxter Park Terrace, from 1885
The west side of the park was lined with a long row of upmarket tenements for mill gaffers, each ennobled by a title – **Singleton Place**, **Pretoria Place**, etc. Bay-windowed and three-dimensional in a Glaswegian manner in contrast to so much of Dundee's plain two-dimensional blocks. **1–3** by McCulloch & Jamieson have finer details than the others.

Below *Baxter Park pavilion.*
Bottom *The opening ceremony of the Park, 1863, from the* Illustrated London News

92 **Baxter Park**, 1863
Dundee's best formal Victorian park, the result of the donation of £50,000 from David Baxter and his sisters, who invited Sir Joseph Paxton, in 1859, to advise on layout; nothing but the best would do. The upper end of the park is laid out formally, with the pleasant Renaissance pavilion forming the transition to the more open space downhill. The **pavilion**, by Paxton's

son-in-law, G H Stokes, has a loggia of twin Doric columns and contains a niche for the marble statue of Sir David by Sir John Steell, 1863 (now in the McManus Galleries). Badly vandalised, the pavilion's last night may fast approach. Opposite the principal promenade of Baxter Park, **69 Dalkeith Road** (former manse), 1890, C & L Ower, is an eccentric essay in red stone medievalism, steep roofs, tall spiral chimneypots, finials, carvings etc. Surrounding railings central to the design.

93 **Anchorage**, 8 Bingham Terrace, C & L Ower Less Gothic and more seafaring, as befits its name: the hall has a Corinthian-columned screen, and there is an outlook on the roof. **6 Bingham Terrace**, 1907, J Foggie, has a turn- of-the-century domed roof. The remainder of Bingham Terrace seems like a Muswell Hill transplant: a row of semi-detached houses, 1909, Hutton & Tough, with timberwork balconies, verandahs, turrets: their external skin consists of harled expanded metal lath.

Eastern Necropolis, Craigiebank
Notable for its triple-arched Gothic gateway in oiled stone, with curving traceried walls, 1863, by W Scott & D Mackenzie.

Taybank Works, Arbroath Road, 1873, was built by Pearce Brothers as a spinning mill attached to an earlier weaving shed. Elaborate cast-iron roof. Distinctive 1949 extension in brick and faïence by SCWS architect Kenneth Masson, is one of only two active jute mills built in the 20th century. Its chamfered corner and recessed entrance is a direct descendant of the 1930s.

Top *69 Dalkeith Road exterior and interior*. Above *Eastern Necropolis*. Below *Church of the Latter Day Saints, Bingham Terrace by Thoms & Wilkie*. Right *Taybank Works*

Wallace Craigie Works
Still used by the family firm William Halley & Sons, a fireproof mill of 1834–6 extended during

the American Civil War. Rare survival of chimney stack complete with cornice. Board-room was originally a hand-loom weaving shop.

82–86 Broughty Ferry Road, 1890, C & L Ower
Model tenement with applied Florentine details built for shipbuilder Henry Gourlay whose Camperdown Shipyard it overlooked.

Watson Street Housing, 1981,
DDC Architects
The characteristic Dundonian severity of the restored tenements stands as a yardstick of what this colourful fishing-village was attempting to flee. Such East-Neukery seems more appropriate to the steepness of this slope and the views over the docks to the firth than further into town.

THE ROUTE EAST
The coastal route east from Dundee formed part of the route from Aberdeen to Edinburgh. Few survivals of ancient history, inner dominated by dock and industrial developments, outer by the opulent grandeur of West Ferry, the ancient fishing village of Broughty, Barnhill and Monifieth.

Top *1946 house in Bingham Terrace.*
Above *Watson Street housing*

Roodyards Burial Ground,
Broughty Ferry Road
Receptacle for 1561 plague victims. Most monuments date 1820–60, an exception being the elaborate domed 18th-century Guthrie mausoleum, with its blind arches and paired Ionic pilasters. Catacomb by the rear gate.

Guthrie mausoleum, Roodyards Burial Ground

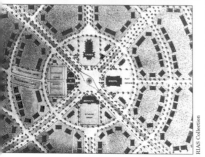

95 **Carolina House**, 1870, William Chalmers
Built on the cliff edge as the Orphan
Institution (to replace the original in Small's
Wynd), this romantic confection is like a Louis
Napoleon bourgeois villa in the suburbs of
somewhere like Nantes. Towers, turrets, wings,
ironwork and blue-painted stonework makes it
seem like a downbeat public school which, in
its original formation, it was.

Craigiebank, 1919, James & Harry Thomson
Planned as the Craigie Garden Suburb for
artisans, by father and son Thomson, the
concentric layout is its most distinguishing
feature, lifted, as it is, directly from Ebenezer
Howard's *Garden Cities of Tomorrow*. Church
at centre, 1937, by Frank Thomson. Small
blocks of flats designed to resemble self-
contained villas, and many steel shipyard-
houses by Johnston & Baxter.

Top right *Carolina House*. Top
*Mayfield (demolished) by Peddie &
Kinnear in Ferry Road*. Middle
Inside Mayfield. Above *Craigie
Garden Suburb plan*

WEST FERRY
The Craigie Drive roundabout demarks the
western edge of West Ferry. Once one of the
richest suburbs in Europe, it was to here, and
to the slopes above Broughty Ferry, that the
merchant princes and jute barons of Dundee
came to construct their palatial mansions. This
mid-to-late Victorian suburb, embracing some
older, desultory seaside villas along the coast
road, is entirely different in character from the
ancient fishing village of Broughty Ferry
further east.

West Ferry remains private on its plateau
high above the shore: few main roads, minor
ones framed by stone walls and mature trees.
The glimpse of a Tuscan turret above a high
rounded coping will have to suffice for many
West Ferry houses. They may be stylistically
various but, basking restlessly as they do
behind their tall walls, they share most
essentials. They are fundamentally long and
horizontal, rather than vertical; similar in
plan – often entered through the gable

Alexander Johnston established
his own practice in 1869 after
working with Peddie & Kinnear on
the Morgan Hospital and Mayfield.
His firm later became Johnston &
Baxter, and its successor, Baxter
Clark & Paul, is one of the largest
architectural practices in Scotland.

(usually porticoed) into a sumptuous north-facing stair-hall frequently with a large fireplace, seating, and lit by large stained glass windows behind the staircase. Many have projecting billiard rooms or conservatories (or both). Points of fundamental similarity are greater than points of visual difference. There is none of the vertiginous baronial homogeneity of King's Park or Bridge of Allan (see *Stirling & The Trossachs* in this series), nor the bourgeois placidity of, say, Grange (see *Edinburgh* in this series), or Bearsden, Glasgow. What matters here, in this stylistic fruit salad where money could buy anything (Peterhead granite to French mural painters) except intellectual rigour, is the skyline: frequently undigested and spikily bombastic – probably similar to the occupiers themselves. There is an undertow of American suburbanism in the vigour with which all this is carried out – to begin with by James Maclaren, then considerably more transatlantic by J Murray Robertson, moving into an Arts & Crafts with Freeman & Ogilvy.

Below *Claypotts Castle*. Bottom *Claypotts as it was in 1854*

Claypotts, 1560–88
Erected by John Strachan during the period troubled by the throw-back predator, Henry Lovell of Ballumbie, who was terrorising the neighbourhood from the fastness of his château just to the north. Strachan clearly sought to erect a villa at which, in the words of Forbes of Corgarff *thieves will need knock ere they durst enter*. The result is this robust structure, two swelling round towers flanking the central block. Apparently the apotheosis of the Z-plan

Rolls-Royces were said to cluster more thickly in West Ferry than anywhere else in the United Kingdom during the 1930s. Perhaps it was because Robertson, the taxi tycoon, would consider few other makes of automobile for his fleet of cabs (eg. the Belgian Minervas).

(although in detail the remnant of Wester Powrie is altogether better), Claypotts is characterised by its two towers capped with square, oversailing attic storeys of a dumpy and disproportionate sort, corbelled out from below. The building was constructed over at least a twenty-year period (Pont indicates the side towers lower and flat in 1592), which may account for the changes in the way it was constructed so visible in its masonry now that its harling has been removed. Turrets have been sliced off; strangely truncated parapet walks, perhaps originally intended to run all the way round, were later roofed in when the money ran out. Principal rooms on the first floor above vaulted storey and kitchens. Scant detail, although one of the four dormer window-heads that survive is decorated with a Renaissance sunburst. *Ancient Monument, open to the public; guidebook available*

97 **Craigiebarn**, Craigiebarn Road, 1911, C G Soutar (colour page 108)
A Scots response to English Arts & Crafts – rubbly with harling, boarded gables and a conservatory. Entered through a low archway and sunken porch, the house's interior opens up into a brilliant first-floor apartment with good plasterwork: it runs the entire length of the house with oriel windows to the firth. Just behind, **Northern College**, off Gardyne Road, 1974, Thoms & Wilkie, has clean-cut geometric shapes to suit its site, and a superb theatre.

The Wyck, Craigie Drive, 1908, Freeman & Ogilvy
Arts & Crafts with a Scots accent: white harled with stone dressings, ashlar chimney stacks, tile-hung gables and an enclosed verandah. The client, J G Lees, was clearly an Anglophile if not Anglo himself. The architects apparently regretted *that circumstances compelled their departure from the traditional Scottish style, and deprecate[d] the introduction of the prettiness of the south.*

Below *The Wyck*. Bottom *Northern College*

98 **Sunningdale**, 2 Ralston Road, 1933,
Donald Ross of Thoms & Wilkie (colour page 108)
Striking, flat-roofed villa whose fretted
parapet is a response to the Algerian
preferences of the client. Strong visual
similarity in the recessed centre between
Sunningdale and the Behrens house in
Northampton. Details very sparse: everything
in the geometry and the modelling. Its
neighbour was (before defenestration) another
1930's fashion plate: brick, string-courses, jazz
glass, canopies and a swelling two-storeyed
bow with horizontal windows.

Beachtower, Ralston Road, 1875,
J Murray Robertson
Like the houses in Court Street, constructed
from shuttered concrete, then masked with
stucco, Greek and Italianate details.

9 **Northwood**, 118 Strathern Road, 1880–2,
G S Aitken, extended 1911, Robert Gibson
Huge towered mansion built for the nabob
Mudies, now converted into the headquarters of
the Servite Housing Association; in whose
grounds now stand sheltered housing and a
mews development alongside the Strathern
Road wall with the characteristic crisp
Scandinavian detail, colour and fondness for
roofscape of J F Stephen. 17th- and 18th-
century in period, plasterwork, glowing
timberwork, marbled chimneypieces and
columns, stained glass, etc, albeit a case of
buying style without rigour. **Hermon Lodge**,
1870, Charles Edward: pleasant Italianate
tower: spectacular domed conservatory. (colour
page 108)

Top *Beachtower*. Above *Northwood*

Balnacraig

Balnacraig, 30 Albany Road, 1863,
(?)James Maclaren
Another homage to Queen Victoria's Osborne
House on the Isle of Wight: three-storey

141

Italianate flat-topped tower lords it over a two-storey house with white painted margins. Typically lavish for a Dundonian bourgeoisie – columned and pilastered hall and staircase, balustraded stair and stained glass window in the hall. In the garden lurks **Lazarim**, 1982, Nicoll Russell Studio – brilliant black-and-white, half of whose gable is glazed to the eaves. Chimney stack and balustrade both infected by crow-steppery.

The Croft, 5 Albany Road, 1898, J Murray Robertson

Some croft! Red brick, red tiles covered in trellis, otherwise a busy design all roofs and chimneys in the American manner, built for 100 H B Gilroy. **Claremont**, 61 Albany Road, re-modelled 1921, W B D Keith, was re-fashioned into a great marmalade mansion for William Boyd of Keillers. Interior plasterwork – notably the billiard room – and glowing mahogany woodwork throughout the spacious hall and staircase, are sumptuous. **Albany Lodge**, 47 Grove Road, is a delightful classical box, with Ionic columns and a lunette laughing where there should have been a pediment. Thomson's assistant at the Caird Hall, Vernon Constable, is said to have had a hand in it.

Fairfield, Fairfield Road, c.1868, is the last West Ferry survivor of Perth architect Andrew Heiton's mansions: sweeping slated roofs, and rows of tall plate-glass windows. Conservatory.

Top *Lazarim*. Middle *Albany Lodge*. Above *Fairfield*

Invergarry, 10 Fairfield Road, 1903, Holt & Glover

Prominent swept red-tiled roofs of Liverpool Arts & Crafts with a conservatory: notable for its rows of tall casement plate-glass windows. **Redcourt**, 17 Fairfield Road, 1886, Hippolyte Blanc (completed G G MacLaren), stands out by its thumping heavily detailed red sandstone, confident Renaissance detailing, tall chimney stacks and high French roofs.

Inveravon

Inveravon, 2a Ellislea Road, 1877 later home of David C Thomson, the newspaper magnate, was designed by James Maclaren and George Shaw Aitken. Distinctive entrance porch with pilasters and ogival roof, and wonderful conservatory. **Moyness**, 76 Grove Road, 1876, another villa by J Murray Robertson, camouflages how he exploited the possibilities of the shuttered concrete he used for the

structure. **Ballinard**, corner Davidson Street, 1871, G S Aitken, is vigorous Gothic built for Watson of Watson's Bond. Mummified within later hotel alterations are its barge-boarding, Germanic towers and splendid timber-balconied west façade.

Dundee Road

A number of villas opening right and left from the road running along the raised beach above the Tay. The Gothic **Lodge, 65**, designed by Andrew Heiton, 1866, as the entrance to (demolished) Fernhall for flax-spinner John Sharp is typical L-plan with a round entrance tower etc. **Taycliff, 20**, 1862, Edward & Robertson, is generally French with a fish-scale and diamond-patterned slate roof. **Harecraig, 26**, c.1835(?), George Mathewson, possibly the dower house of the Douglas & Angus Estate, and extruded, 1911, by Mills & Shepherd in every direction to break up the regularity, became home of architect Charles G Soutar, 1928–47, who altered the drawing room and added a 17th-century-style chimneypiece incorporating some old Persian tiles. **Magdala, 32**, 1930, Bruce, Son & Morton was commissioned by the Lord Provost, Sir James Urquhart, seeking to escape from Roseangle. Generally Arts & Crafts with a Westmorland slate roof: art deco chimneypiece within. The **Royal Tay Yacht Club** (Fort William), **34**, 1838, George Mathewson, is very seasidey: two octagonal bays flanking Ionic-columned verandah, upper storey pedimented above.

Royal Tay Yacht Club (colour p.125)

95 Dundee Road, 1964, James Parr

The architect's own house platformed out from the sylvan grounds of his office garden and entered from the side. The hall downstairs takes the form of a central well, which can be merged with the dining room when required. Better view from the drawing room upstairs. Lovely timberwork.

Drawing room, 95 Dundee Road

143

Above *Aystree*. Right *Interior*

Aystree, 26 Victoria Road, 1903, Charles Ower & Charles Soutar

Arts & Crafts with hungry masonry, mullioned windows, eaves, chimney stacks, Doric-columned entrance, strapwork, etc. Exceptional interior retaining original light fixtures, bathroom ceramics, door furniture. Oak-panelled hall, Liberty-patterned stencilling, panelled cloakroom, ingle-nook, fitted library and beamed ceiling in the dining room.

BROUGHTY FERRY

Broughty Ferry is to Dundee what Portobello was to Edinburgh: the nearest available seaside resort, with the added attraction of an élite enclave on rising land behind. A fishing village had long sheltered around the castle-protected harbour, called Partan Craig, but Regency seagoing soon transformed that. In 1801, a feuing plan was drawn up for the *new town at the North Ferry*, parts of which incorporated older buildings in King Street and Brook Street. A further feuing plan, drawn up by David Neave in 1825 on the lands of the feu superior General Charles Hunter of Burnside,

Broughty Ferry from the south. Visible on the hill behind are Carbet Castle (centre) and Castleroy (top right)

proposed a grid-iron layout based upon King Street and Queen Street. The place swiftly became fashionable, to the extent that **St Aidan's Church**, 408 Brook Street, James Black, was opened in May 1826 principally to serve summer visitors. A few years later, a chronicler recorded that the Ferry, *of very late origin, is rapidly increasing. It owes its rise to having become a fashionable resort for sea bathing. The sea water here is very pure, with a clean sloping beach. The village is built upon dry sand, which in some places is blown by the wind; and it admits of unlimited extension ... Besides the resort for sea bathing, which only takes place during the summer, weavers and mechanics are building houses and settling here.* In 1838–9 the railway arrived. Lord Cockburn, on one of his Circuit Journeys, thought Broughty Ferry decidedly superior to Portobello because it was *backed by a high rising ground ... on which are perched an increasing variety of good gardened houses, some of which are obviously excellent mansions ... but it wants the glorious Portobello sands ...*

01 **Broughty Castle**, begun *c*.1490
A seat of Andrew, second Lord Gray, Broughty was of strategic importance, governing harbour and ferry point of Port-on-Craig (thought to be Partan Craig, or Crab Rock), since its controller commanded the Tay. The castle consisted of a large rectangular tower, with substantial outworks and high fortified enclosure, with towers at the corner. Occupied by the English in 1547 (during which time they erected a fort on Balgillo Hill from which stranglehold they harried the countryside for the next two years) it was recovered in 1550, only to be besieged nine years later by the Lords of the Congregation and then in turn by the Catholics. The castle, latterly the home of Master of Gray, does not appear to have been occupied much after the 17th century – although it was still entire in 1716. By 1821, when offered for sale, it was wholly ruinous – misleadingly advertised on the basis that it could be *repaired at small expense ... and would make an excellent situation for an inn.*

The 1861 repairs by R Rowand Anderson for the War Office, became a virtual reconstruction – so much so as to be referred to as the *new castle.* Purists such as David MacGibbon and Thomas Ross gave up upon the building

Our auld ynemies of England, as the Privy Council Minute has it, *being in the hous of Bruchtie, ar apperandly to invaid the burc of Dundie and haill cuntre, and to burn, herey, sla and destroy etc.*

Broughty Castle from the air

Walker

As a Victorian strongpoint, Broughty Castle was not a success. Lecturing on the defence of the Tay, in 1888, Captain J G Grant described the castle as *badly built, badly designed, and utterly useless for the purpose for which it was constructed ... A fort such as this could never defend our river, for its total demolition would only afford an enemy an hour's pleasant and agreeable recreation, un-harassed by any thoughts of possible danger to themselves.*

McKean

Dundee Public Libraries

Top Broughty Ferry seafront. Above The Ferry when still a fishing village

Fisher Street

Wishart

altogether. Anderson's task was to provide a small military outpost to control the Tay, which he did by *restoring* the square tower into a partially harled L-shaped one, replacing all traces of the outworks with picturesque but inefficient mid-Victorian fortifications, moated and draw-bridged. Now a branch museum – to Broughty Ferry, whaling and fish. *Open to the public*. **Castle Green** has a particularly well-equipped children's playground. Once home of a fishing fleet, the location of the first roll-on, roll-off ferries in Britain, and home of a submarine mine unit of the Victorian volunteers, the **Harbour** is used entirely for leisure.

Fisher Town

The shoreside portion of Broughty Ferry enjoys that indefinable seaside atmosphere of seabirds and breeze. Within its grid-iron layout, you can enjoy the quiet spaciousness of historic, small-scale buildings comforting each other against the elements, the attractive proximity of the sea at the foot of each street, and the swelling of the main thoroughfares with Victorian commerce. **Brook Street**, with its three churches – the Gothic **Congregational**, 1864, James Maclaren; the cruciform **St Stephen's**, 1871, T S Robertson (good Morris & Company glass inside); and **St Aidan's** – is *downtown Ferry*. There is also the 1825 **YMCA** (former school room), the 19th-century (former) **Municipal Buildings** with its wrought-iron arch and clock, and the neoclassical **Masonic Hall**, 1911, H & F Thomson, with its lavish Edwardian paintings and plasterwork. **Bayne & Duckett**, 1977, by Nicoll Russell Studio is *architecture parlante* – an elephantine bronzed glass representation of a boot. In **King Street**, 156 has an early shopfront, and the late 18th-century **Eagle Inn**, 155–159, an 1860 eagle by James Law on the south wall. Tall 1987 housing by the Parr Partnership in brown brick and sweeping roofs contrasts to the white purity of delightful **Agnes Square**, 1974.

Left *King Street*. Above *Bayne & Duckett*. Below *Agnes Square*. Middle *Fisher Street barometer case (and dog)*. Bottom *Doorway, Gray Street*

Links House, 357 King Street, c.1825, style of David Neave
The loveliest classical house in the Ferry (despite what they have tried to do to its windows). Plainly elegant, with steps rising over basement to a Doric-columned entrance with fanlight.

102 The Shore begins with **Douglas Terrace**, pleasant ashlar semi-detached villas, 1838, designed by George Mathewson who lived in a humbler one just to the west of the bridge.
1–13 James Place, a neoclassical terrace with chased stonework and curved corners, leads into **Fisher Street**, 115 having a Negretto & Zambia 1859 barometer in its stone case in its wall. **Bellrock Square**, 1973, James Parr & Partners, continued the fishing aesthetic with harled walls, coloured window surrounds and a variegated roofscape.

Beach Crescent comprises good 19th-century
103 seaside villas, launched by the **Red House**, 99 Beach Crescent. The Red House was General Hunter's own: two-storey, bow-fronted U-plan villa, red-harled with stone margins if otherwise plain. The bow indicates a delightful oval room with original plasterwork and fireplace, giving on to the sea. **9–13** Beach Crescent, c.1800 are harled with margins. Wonderfully opulent fanlight to **Gray Street**. **Beach House**, c.1825, were two classical town houses married c.1860 – pedimented doors, fanlights, architraves etc.

31 Beach Crescent, 1866, James Maclaren
A vaguely Italianate villa designed for Stephens (the shipbuilder whose firm built Captain Scott's *Discovery*), it was converted to the **Orchar Gallery** to display the splendid collection of 19th-century Scots paintings (comprising the largest group of the Scott Lauder School of Painting) bequeathed by

147

Robertson & Orchar, from which James Guthrie Orchar (see p. 130) derived his wealth, provided a full design and build service including structural castings and the provision of mill machinery. He was an important patron of the Arts for the last 30 years of his life, purchasing pictures mainly by MacTaggart and the Scott Lauder Group, together with etchings by Whistler & Seymour Hayden. At least one painting by Whistler had to be sold to meet his numerous bequests and annuities. He was an important figure in the Dundee musical world, owning a Stradivarius and other important violins, acting as host to the violinist, Joachim, when he came to Dundee. The creation of the Orchar Gallery was specified in his will, but was not implemented until 1921 since his widow had life rent of his estate. Her nephew, David Douglas, sold the violins to build up the collection further, probably on lines discussed with his uncle.

Provost J Guthrie Orchar. Orchar originally intended his gallery for a new building in Reres Park, but only got as far as completing the 1897 gateway. After barely 60 years of independent existence, the collection now embellishes the McManus Galleries in Albert Square. Now a nursing home.

An engaging mixture of 18th- and 19th-century houses and cottages in the cross streets, some one, some two-storey; some stone, some harled and some stucco; some slate, some tiles – with an increasingly freewheeling and undisciplined use of corbels, chimneys, doorcases, dormers, roofs and gables as the century progresses. **Fort Street** is the best. **St James Church**, 1889, Edward & Robertson, with adjacent fishermen's reading room, 1896, and 1907 hall by D W Baxter is generally Romanesque. **Fisherman's Tavern**, 10, is early 19th century painted and rendered. **32–34** Fort Street, is like a late 18th-century Improvement farm house (which perhaps it was) – three-bay two-storey with keystoned door and cornice. **83–86** Fort Street, 1885, retains the original florid shopfronts. In **Gray Street**, a white-boarded railway signal box tower with florid cast-iron is a relic of the 1838 arrival of railways – in the days when they were exuberant and fun.

Catholic Church, Westfield Road

Wishart

Queen Street is the main artery of the Ferry with more churches (Ferry holidaymakers must have been an observant crowd). **St Luke's**, 1884, H J Blanc, possibly the best: originally a Free Church, it is confident, red sandstone and cruciform with good Morris & Company glass in the apse. It was built by a breakaway congregation professing an unusual fondness for church music (colour page 125). 104 **St Mary's Episcopal**, 1858, Sir George Gilbert Scott, is unpretentious on the exterior. *The Ecclesiologist*'s inspector spent little time inspecting (like so many juries); contenting himself with a glimpse as he whizzed past by train, sufficient to conclude that it was *a simple specimen of correct ecclesiology*. He missed its rather beautiful interior whose chancel was lengthened by Sir Robert Lorimer, 1911. **Guliston House** (restaurant and snooker club) was once the **Queen Street Church**, 1876, James Maclaren & G S Aitken – well proportioned, striped stone gables, tall western tower and semi-hexagonal chancel facing east. Some stained glass remains. The **East Church**, 1865, Andrew Heiton, has fish-

Public Library

Wishart

scale roofs with fleur-de-lis finials, buttresses and other Gothic details. Characteristically Dundonian unfinished tower. The **Public Library**, 1928, James M Brown, is a pleasant single-storey version of the Petit Trianon, pilastered central bay projecting, extended 1970s by City Architect, Dundee Corporation.

Herschel House, 8–10 Hill Street, *c.*1827 has pleasant Regency south façade with projecting central bay, cast-iron balustrade to entrance steps, and original interiors. **Dunalistair**, 21 Hill Street, mid 19th century, displays Italianate Victorianism overwhelming General Hunter's earlier villa. Latterly holiday home for families of The Black Watch; now flats.

McKean

Walker

Left *Interior of Dunalistair.*
Above *Whinnybrae*

VC House, 21 Hill Street, *c.*1880
Billiard room of Dunalistair House converted into self-contained residence, 1984, with all the lavishness that a billiard room commanded: pilasters, Corinthian capitals, balustraded parapet and magnificent marbled interior.

Whinnybrae, 1911, Langlands and Lamond Former Eastern School in creamy stone with Lamond's characteristic lanterns in the roof, large semicircular windows in the gable, and wavy parapet to the two flanking stair-towers. 105 **Camphill Road**, the ancient route to Monifieth, has a number of good villas. **Loftus**

House, 16, and **St Margaret's**, 18, are both late Regency – the former with a bow front and Greek Ionic porch, 1835, the latter Italianised. **Camphill House**, 50, 1850, James Maclaren, is neo-Jacobean in painted stone. **The Bughties**, 76, 1882, J Murray Robertson, conceals a rigorous symmetry behind half-timbering, red tiles and tall brick chimney stacks with a transatlantic hard- edged verve. Sadly, the site is over-developed.

Top *Hill Street*. Middle *Camphill House*. Above *The Bughties*. Right *The Bughties elevation*

The amazing fairytale Hampton Court skyline of **Castleroy** was erected in 1867 by Andrew Heiton for the Gilroy dynasty, demolished following an attack of dry rot, and only its delightful Tudor gatehouse closing Hill Street survives.

At **7 Camphill Road** lay Castleroy's rival, **Carbet Castle**, of which the baronial gate lodge alone survives. The Grimonds kept on extending an earlier house in eccentric style in measure to the size of the rival dynasty's

Below *Carbet Castle lodge*. Right *The hall at Castleroy (demolished)*

palace designed mainly by T S Robertson. Its
interior was lavish to a degree: painted ceilings
by Charles Fréchou survive, one entombed
within the Matthew Building (see p.80). Dry
rot, being even handed, did for the Grimonds as
for the Gilroys. (colour page 125)

BARNHILL

More grand mansions intermixed with lesser.
Reres House, 1849, is a barge-boarded
cottage mansion of the sort normally favoured
by David Bryce. Unobtrusive, pleasant white
housing in **Strathmore Street**, 1974, is by
Baxter Clark & Paul. **Bonspiel Gardens**,
1974, Mercer Blaikie is a cul-de-sac of harled
cottages. **2–4 Invermark Terrace** has
unusual stone details. **St Margaret's**, 1895,
Duncan Carmichael, is an unfinished church
in Scots Gothic; begun as an established

Top *Castleroy (demolished)*. Middle
*Saloon in Carbet Castle
(demolished)*. Above *Strathmore
Street*. Left *St Margaret's Church*

church for the Revd Newbiggin Adamson, until
he was prosecuted at the General Assembly by
the Revd Jacob Primmer of Dunfermline for
holding Sunday Service so early as to be
tainted by Episcopalianism. Everyone aspired
to **Panmure Terrace**: the **Gorse**, No 11,
1800, extended by James Maclaren;
Rowanlee, No 15, *c.*1865 by James Maclaren
in Italianate mode; **Ferncroft**, 6a Panmure
Terrace, 1913, Thoms & Wilkie, harled with
stone margins beneath red tiles and extended,
1990, by Nicoll Russell Studio; and
Longcroft, 2 Panmure Terrace, 1922,
Maclaren Soutar & Salmond, in good English
Edwardian – with tall panelled brick
chimneys, loggia, hipped roof and Doric portico
to the garden.

MONIFIETH

Village and parish in its own right which
became industrial surprisingly early. By 1845,
the village of thatched cottages with its ancient

Longcroft

Top *Grange House*. Above *19th-century reconstruction of the vitrified broch on the Laws of Monifieth*

church and beautifully carved antique tombstones, was dominated by *a somewhat extensive iron foundry*. Monifieth's glories lie in the hill looking south-east over the sea, and the late-Victorian villas which swarmed over them.

St Rule's Parish Kirk, 1813, Samuel Bell
Plain but conspicuous (having to make do with the square bell tower instead of its proposed spire) this classically proportioned but Gothic detailed kirk (with memorial glass by Morris & Company) has a gallery on cast-iron classical columns within its Gothic skin. It incorporates a 1626 aisle of the Durhams of Pitkerro. The **Manse**, 1829, David Mackenzie, has giant angle pilasters and a Doric portico. Curious Grecian ornamentation – architraves, dentils, balustrades – has been lavished upon the stucco cottage at **4 Hill Street**.

Grange House, 1829, James Black
Attractive, almost Italianate villa whose rusticated stone quoins contrast with harling: horizontal in proportion. Harmony now has to be detected beneath the re-glazing, the encroachment of other building, and luxuriant overgrowth which conceals the sumptuous 17th-century Renaissance gate piers to the former Grange of Monifieth (demolished). The **Bone House**, The Laws, 1836, was probably erected to contain the results of nearby excavations.

James Maclaren, the master of the suburban seat, was the dominant designer of 19th-century Monifieth. He was architect to the Panmure Estate, and those developing sites in Barnhill or Monifieth had to commission him. His was the Gothic T-plan **South Church**, 1872; **Seaview**, Hill Street, 1860 – a sprawling Jacobean villa with hood-moulds, heraldic panel, string-course, dormers and tower; nearby **Viewfirth**, smaller and plainer; **Tighnudin**, Queen Street, 1874, vigorously gabled and be-chimneyed; and **Ashlea**, Victoria Street, 1870, in a form of neoclassical. Of these, possibly the most opulent is **Ashludie**, Victoria Street, 1866: an overblown version of Camphill House in sprawling Jacobean. Gables, shaped chimneys, corbels, heraldic panels, etc, provided gentility for the flax-spinning client, embellished with walled garden and conservatory. Running it close, however, is **Tigh-na-Muir**, 1893, J M Robertson, a

Milton House Hotel: Left *Elevation.*
Above *Cross section*

miniature Panmure House, a smart and
powerful U-plan house in crisp ashlar, with
French windows, balcony and ogee-roofed stair-
towers.

Milton House Hotel, 1912, Thoms & Wilkie
Remodelling of an older mill house into Grange
Cottage: the transformation of a plain late 18th-
century three-bay house just apparent beneath
its kilt of 17th-century Scots – harled, crow-
steps, dressings and dormer windows.

DUNDEE HINTERLAND
This section is divided into three parts beyond
the common inner boundary of Kingsway/
Arbroath Road: first, east of **Forfar Road**;
second between **Forfar Road** and **Coupar
Angus Road**; and lastly west of **Coupar
Angus Road**. The north-west/south-east valley
of the River Dichty cuts across each with its
riparian communities, dams, mills, bleachfields
and viaducts. The countryside is of an
extraordinary beauty the further west. Rural
Scotland of the loveliest kind laps up the very
fringes of the city, with quiet communities and
peaceful country lanes.

Panmure Bleachfield, Balmossie, from 1839
Bleach did not always come in packets. It was
its own industry – and these relics of a
bleaching complex comprise **manager's house**
(later tenement), access bridge, four single-
storey bleachfield cottages (quite smart –
harled with dressings); and nearby 18th-
century **Balmossie Mill**, which probably
cannibalised the medieval Chapel of St Andrew
on the opposite bank of the Dichty.

Linlathen East Bridge, 1795–1810
Nothing now remains of the seat of Burns'
friend Graham of Fintry. The East Bridge, built
in the policies probably to provide direct access

*Outer north-east Dundee c.1592
drawn by Timothy Pont. No roads:
dominated by rivers with a dense
concentration of country houses.
Clock-wise from bottom left is Mains
(shown near Craigie, and not the
Mains Castle we know today),
Kirkton of Mains, Maidiens (almost
certainly the Mains Castle as we
know today), Strathmartine Castle
and Kirkton, Baldovie, Claverhouse,
Wester Powrie, bottom right, above
the word Whitfield, is Ballumbie*

Top *Unsuccessful design by James Playfair for the reconstruction of Baldovie House*. Right *Ballumbie Castle*

Auld Ballumbie, otherwise Henry Lovell of Ballumbie, used his castle as the base to prey upon his neighbours (and his son) in the mid 16th century. In 1566, the rather wet James Durham of Pitkerro complained to the Queen about the *manifest oppression* which had forced him to flee from *his own house, and dare nocht resort thereto neither by day nor nicht and stands continually under fear and danger of his life.* Twenty years later, Auld Ballumbie was still irritating the authorities, this time by burning the minister of Monifieth from his manse.

Popular doggerel records another Lovell family trait:
Come I late, or come I air Ballumbie's board's aye bare.

Ballumbie House (now ruinous)

to the steading without going past the house, is the oldest iron bridge in Scotland, and one of the oldest in the world. Single cast-iron arch has spandrels of roundels which diminish in size towards the centre, with the parapet of quatrefoils. Stone buttresses. The 1830 **West Bridge** is similar, but with smart corniced stone buttresses. Perhaps the transparency of the earlier one affrighted the ladies.

Michelin Athletic Club, Baldovie, 1734
Harled two-storeyed crow-stepped house with later entrance tower, much of its façade concealed by later additions. Sadly, it escaped transmogrifying in smart neoclassical by locally born architect, James Playfair. Nearby 1789 **Toll House** harled with margins.

107 **Ballumbie Castle**, Ballumbie Road, from 14th century
Much ruined remnant of what was probably (to judge from the large, finely margined windows) a sophisticated château, of which only a curtain wall and two round towers now survive capping a raised mound, protected by a burn. Ruined since records began, it became the stable court for now roofless Georgian **Ballumbie House**, which was converted to Scots revivalism, 1902, by James Findlay. Once lavish – harled with stone margins, Caithness slate roof, crow-steps, hood-moulds and corbels. Fine chimneypieces survive within the ruins.

108 **Pitkerro**, 1593, extended 1902, Robert Lorimer
Long rectangular country house (which Durham re-built post-Ballumbie?) with customary ground floor, circular stair-tower, principal floor with large windows, and steps up to corner turrets or gazebos. Top floor dormered; stair-tower corbelled out to become a study.

Pitkerro

Transmogrified into the servants' wing from an Edwardian mansion in 17th-century Scots, the new house overwhelming the original, to which Lorimer restored the roof pitch, stair turret, and dormer windows (although altering the ground floor). He wrote: *been at my Pitkerro job all day. I always want to get another job in exactly the same style when I have done one. If I got a very large and purely domestically treated Scotch house today, now with the experience I have had of that, I think I could give it beans. There is nothing in the world for teaching one like having to turn out the work.* Good Lorimer plan and detail – decorative plasterwork, panelling etc. Contemporary bulbous Lorimer **lodge**. **Pitkerro Mill**, 1583 rebuilt 1812, converted to a house, retains its overshot wheel. Lovely gardens.

Duntrune House, 1826, William Burn
Graceful classical house in Tudor overcoat, given style and skyline by its shafted chimneys. Policies include terrace, ha-ha, bee-boles and sweeping entrance gates. Upmarket cottages at Burnside of Duntrune: contemporary, and perhaps by Burn. The 1848 **aqueduct** by harbour engineer, James Leslie, carried water for Dundee over the Fithie Burn. Other aqueducts are at Gagie. The ruined 1826 grain mill was fed by the horseshoe weir.

Duntrune House

Highbroom, 1924, Mills & Shepherd
Fusion of late-Scots revival with Arts & Crafts: harled with stone dressings, towers, corbels, swept roofs, moulded doorway and pestiferous red tiles.

Murroes House, from mid 16th century
Timothy Pont's 1592 map implies Murroes was then a three-storeyed crow-stepped house, but

perhaps he got a storey wrong. Built by the Fothringhams of Wester Powrie, it looks like a dower house. After neglect, harling stripped off and roof cut back, it was restored from agricultural slumdom in 1942. Rectangular two-bay house with central chimney and projecting stair, crow-stepped gables and forestair to court. Pantomime gunloops. 1859 panelling within, taken from David Bryce's demolished Fothringham House. Court with outbuildings including larder. 17th-century **doocot** in the farm. **Farm steading**, 1793, follows immediately upon the 1792 Montgomery Act which allowed lairds (in this case the Guthries of Gagie) to offset costs of improvement against their entail rather than revenue. Single-storeyed court perhaps incorporating earlier farm at the centre of the west range. Adjacent **mill** (now ruinous) has its own steading.

Murroes Parish Kirk, 1848, William Scott T-plan Gothic upon an ancient site, incorporating an earlier burial vault and stones and relics from its predecessor – heraldic panel, shields, jougs and 1642 north aisle. The Minister in the late 17th century was the Revd Robert Edward, author of the idiosyncratic *Description of the County of Angus*, 1678, and father of Andrew Edward who, at one point, was assistant to Sir William Bruce. Some fine tombs including table tombs, carved relics and 18th-century coach house.

Gagie House: Below Summer house. Middle Grange of Gagie re-using the Scott Street Church roof. Bottom Stables

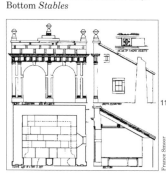

111 **Gagie House**, Gagie, 1614, restored by France Smoor
The turreted gable of this petite mock-military country house (dower house for Guthrie) projects into its walled garden, as guardian of the delightful two-bay Doric **summer house**, a garderobe in the far corner of the garden, and the fine 17th-century baluster sun-dial. Its long rectangular form forms a group with Murroes, Pitkerro and Wester Fowlis. Much extended in

Clare Smoor

the later 18th century (the coach house is 1579), it has been repeatedly reconstructed after fire. The present owners have restored the stables and summer house, the main house, the garden cottage, gate lodge and laundry in a continuous programme of work. To the complex they have added the **Grange**, a new brick and block building with turrets re-using a church roof.

Affleck or **Auchinleck Castle**, Monikie, late 15th century
Ane old high tower house wrote the 17th-century writer Ochterlony *which is seen at a great distance at sea, and is used for a landmark by those that come in the river of the Tay.* A masterpiece of sound and secure space-planning, Affleck is one of the finest tower house survivals – complete, unpretentious and difficult to visit. A graceful four-storey building with a principal room on each floor, bedrooms, chapel, guardrooms, stairs and garderobes being disposed in the wall's thickness. The great fireplace in the solar has splendidly carved stonework, as has the adjacent barrel-vaulted Chapel which Douglas Simpson considered *singularly beautiful – a perfect little gem.* Allegedly in the custodianship of Historic Scotland. *Guide leaflet; access uncertain.*

Mid Craigie, from 1938,
initially J MacLellan Brown
Dundee's greatest post-war construction lies in the Dichty Valley, saturated by endless estates, generally poor in layout, threadbare in character and spartan in provision. *Per se,* some of the houses are good of their time and type, and suffer only from the paucity of imagination which was applied to developing this dormitory. Along **Fountainbleau Drive**

RCAHMS

Top *Gagie House in snow.*
Above *Affleck Castle*

Top *St Ninian's Church*. Middle *Kingsway Fire Station*. Above *Alloway Terrace*

and **Happyhillock Road** (surely deserving a prize for inappropriate nomenclature) may be seen decent houses of the late 1930s and early 1950s: semi-detached in pinkish brick with horizontal metal windows and wee porches – the layout a bastardisation of Garden City planning. Timber houses around the new primary school in **Rowantree Crescent** deserve to be seen as representative of one period of Scottish building as the fashionable cottars' houses are of another. Much fashionably reclad.

St Ninian's Church, Longtown Road, 1938, Gauldie & Wright
Small harled and buttressed Episcopal church with semi-octagonal window heads, whose elevations reflect the originally proposed structure of diagonally braced timber framing and metal lath. The client preferred something more substantial like brick, but kept the original elevations. **Kingsway East Fire Station**, 1972, is an elegantly geometric essay in brickwork by James Parr & Partners. **Alloway Terrace**, 1976, by Robbie & Wellwood, is a large black-and-white mass of housing like a stranded ocean liner. Note also the student flats of **Alloway Place West**, 1983, Gauldie Wright & Partners, **St Vincent Catholic Church**, 1950s, W W Friskin, and the **Whitfield Catholic Church**, 1973, by James Parr & Partners.

112 **Dunbar Park**, Whitfield, recreated 1989, DDC Architects (colour page 126)
A case of rebuilding a community. The Whitfield Skarne estate was a disastrous system-built experiment of 2500 houses, remote from services and renowned – however unfairly – to be a dumping ground for Dundee's

Below *Whitfield Church*. Right *Whitfield from the air, in the process of transition. The hexagonal plan still dominates, but work has begun*

problems. If it was, the anonymity of the rigid hexagonal plan only exacerbated the problem. The task was to reverse perceptions. By combination of new housing policies, demolition, retrofit, and the introduction of private sector housing so as to remove any stigma, Skarne has become history, and new identities and neighbourhoods have emerged. The distance from town has been alleviated by better buses. **Dunbar Park** was a pioneering £6 million transformation of 381 houses into houses for sale, rent or housing association use, achieved by reduced scale, pitched roofs, new (colourful) elevations, controlled entry systems, defensible space, better thermal performance, landscaping, play areas and flamboyant sculpture. Wonderful for those who like landscape and countryside, although it requires some virginia creeper. Further phases, in association with building societies, housing associations and tenants' groups, include projects by Baxter Clark & Paul, and Hutcheson, Fisher & Campbell.

Dunbar Park: Top left *Dunbar Park*. Top *Butterfly sculpture*. Above *Carberry Crescent*

The Black Watch Memorial, 1959, Scott Sutherland
Bronze Black Watch soldier on sandstone pedestal.

Wester Powrie from the air

13 Wester Powrie, 16th century onwards
Husk of a large château, possibly Z-plan like Claypotts (south-west tower altogether scanty in trace), but considerably more sophisticated in detail, e.g. carving above entrance, splendid first-floor hall with its corbelling, fireplace and large windows. Spacious, almost square private apartment (probably bedroom) in the round tower. East gable and upper storeys vanished. Stood in one corner of a courtyard (*vide* Pont) now almost entirely vanished. The

Wester Powrie: plan of the north wing

north wing, 1604, is a much-altered Renaissance block, whose plan is now difficult to read. Long, rectangular, with square entrance stair-tower corbelled at first floor, with outstanding pilastered and baluster-framed windows. Normal kitchen/bakehouse vaults on ground floor with internal stair up to the principal floor. Two or three apartments and (?)bedroom in the round tower. The east end (which probably abutted another building) inscrutable. Aedicule in west gable. Detail implies a building of much greater importance of which we are seeking but a cut-down relic. Even so, well restored with dormer heads reintroduced by David Leslie.

OUTER NORTH DUNDEE, BETWEEN FORFAR ROAD & COUPAR ANGUS ROAD

[114] **Mains Castle**, Caird Park, 1480–1700
Seat of the Grahams of Fintry since the 16th century pleasantly set on a steep bank above a burn in the Dichty Valley. A courtyard country house built progressively between 1480–1580, it is distinguished by its 70ft-high stair and study tower, and adjacent hall block. Above the boldly carved main entrance there are traces of a linear bartisan (very much like that surviving at Muchalls). Keystone dated 1562, the initials DG and DMO standing for David Graham and Dame Margaret Ogilvy. The castle has a fine Renaissance stone panel with the motto in Latin: *grateful for country, for friends and for posterity*. The principal wing abutting the tower contains a hall, a private chamber and bedrooms above. The unusual corbelled study capping the tower is four

Mains Castle: The study tower drawn in the 19th century

Conjectural restoration by DDC Architects of the entire complex

square, a pediment gable capped by a chimney to each façade, and a window to each airt, offering (like Montaigne's study) a place for contemplation. Reconstructed by DDC Architects as a fine restaurant; harling would have enhanced its vividness. Ecclesiastical (i.e. pedimented) crow-steps introduced in the restoration are unusual in a lay building. (colour page 126)

Old Mains Church, 1800
With its bellcote and horse-shoe gallery, the kirk stands in its own enclosure of stone walls and iron railings, an emblem of continuity in a district much transformed.

Claverhouse Bleachfield, 1835–40
Largest Dundee bleachfield of the early 19th century, founded in the late 18th century and fed by a system of lades, ponds and dams. The bleachfield offices are two-storey with a bellcote, and the *c.*1830 **mansion house**, in the style of James Black, was the home of the chemist Dr Henry Boase, managing partner of the bleachfield. There is a 1780 beating/ beetling house, office and yard, and the most complete 1839 chimney stack left in Dundee. Nearby **Claverhouse Cottages** form a marooned 18th-century village street.

Trottick Mains, comprise rows of harled bleachworkers' cottages, *c.*1800, associated with the Trottick flax spinning mill.

115 **Baldovan House**, Old Glamis Road, mid 18th century
Ruinous grandeur of the former seat of the Ogilvy family (long manufacturers of Dundee). North wing comprises the original Tullideph Hall, utterly transformed *c.*1825, probably by

Below *Mill of Mains.*
Bottom *Claverhouse Cottages*

Baldovan House

The January 1612 contract between Dundee Council and Andrew Wast (mason) specifies the requirements for the construction of Baldovan Millhouse on the Dichty. There is the shadowy intervention of an unspecified Master Mason only in the location of the doors: *Andro Wast, mason ... shall with all possible diligence build one sufficient mill house of stonework at Baldovan, of the length of fifty-two futts within the gables, and the breadth of twenty-two futts within the side walls, which shall be nine feet above the earth and the gables of height proportional. All the walls shall be of thickness two feet and a half foot, if they be built with clay, three feet. Similarly, Andro shall build within the south side wall, in the most commodious place, ane great door of hewen stone of the wideness of twelve feet, and one of the height of the side wall, having the towns arms well hewn above the same, with other two doors in such places as the Master of Work pleases design.*

Sir Robert Smirke with a new south-facing house. Shallow projecting central bay, designed as a triumphal arch, led visitors directly into the *piano nobile* at first floor. Fire-gutted and derelict. Oval walled garden, service wing and stables on the east, 1831. Sundial, 1753.

[116] **Strathmartine Castle**, 1785
Small symmetrical laird's house on (or near) a site of an altogether more splendid affair hazily recorded by Pont: double-bow facing south, its *lang pedigree* evinced by two doocots, one with pyramid roof, the other a lean-to of the 17th century. Pleasant 1791 twin-arched bridge with toll house in Kirkton of Strathmartine.

Strathmartine Parish Church, 1843
Typical post-Disruption church, Norman in style, wheel window c.1900 by David Baxter.

BALDOVAN
The Ogilvys of Baldovan encouraged the development of Downfield and Baldovan suburbs in the mid 19th century, linked by tram from and to the city centre. Communities developed which were self-contained and took pride in their identity.

St Luke's Episcopal, Baldovan Road, 1901, Freeman & Ogilvy
Elegiac church group in pure Scots revival – harled with stone dressings – so well done that it might be 16th century. A small **garden suburb** around Clive Road was promoted, 1929, by Sir Herbert Ogilvy, and designed by London architect W Curtis Green (he of the Dorchester) with Sir Herbert's brother G F M Ogilvy. Unpretentious yet picturesque harled and slated houses, painted in shades of white

Below *Garry Place sheltered housing, DDC Architects, 1985.* Right *Kirkton High School*

and pink, with swept gables, dormer windows and Scots details. Houses in **Ulverston Terrace**, Magdalene Kirkton, 1982, by DDC Architects, attract attention by bright pantiles, swept dormers, black timberwork and harling.

Van Leer Tay, 1946,
Beard, Bennett & Wilkins
A pair with the former Timex Company, designed by the same architects in the same year. Both share characteristics of sweeping brick elevations, thin concrete framed windows and projecting canopies, much in the style of 1930's Dutch architecture. **Timex** introduced production-line technology for watches to Dundee, and constructed a striking headquarters of yellow brick, red sandstone plinth and planters in which massing and scale is everything. Quite distinctly architecture as a marketing tool.

17

Balgray Building (former Olivetti factory), 1971, Edward Cullinan
A most exotic location appropriate for advertising agents. Built as one of a series of experimental buildings for Olivetti, the principal storey of this distinctive structure billows out over the lower, a faintly Chinese

18

Top *Ardler – housing by Baxter Clark & Paul*. Middle *A touch of the Mexicans on Safeway's store, Strathmartine Road*. Above *Van Leer Tay*. Below *Balgray Building courtyard view*. Bottom *Former Timex factory*

Top The 1595 Tealing doocot, in the home farm, has the monogram DM & HG on the lintel. The moulded course is to prevent rats eating pigeons. Above The Iron Age souterrain, or underground earth house (now roofless) which has an 80ft-long curved gallery ending in a small chamber. Ancient Monument; accessible to visitors

impression conveyed by its triangular windows. Largely glazed, curving two-storey façade to the courtyard. Extended by Brunton Voigt. The **Low & Bonar** head office, a striking 1979 piece by Hugh Martin Partnership, has a glass *piano nobile* projecting over a square plinth. (colour page 127)

[119] **Tealing House**, from 17th century
Harled four-bay country house gradually extended north, upgraded in early 18th century, and again by William Burn. South façade in Old Scots, with oculus in pediment and keystone windows. Originally comparable perhaps to Murroes, Pitkerro, Gagie, Powrie etc. Unusual M-gable (see *Ross & Cromarty* in this series). Good interior work. Early 18th-century rectangular walled garden. The **Home Farm** comprises U-plan stable and court, and an L-plan mill complex. Some *c.*1600(?) relics embedded within. Also three crosses and sculptured panels probably from old chapel.

[120] **South Balluderon Farm Steading & Mill**, from 1800
Exceptionally complete agri-business complex of the Napoleonic period, whose survival is attributed to the last farmer's refusal to adapt to tractors. Much original equipment.

Dronley House, 1925, Allan & Friskin
Anachronistic harled Arts & Crafts villa with ashlar dressings, casement mullioned windows, deep eaves beneath a red roof. Notable original interior includes ceilings with floreat plasterwork and stippled paintwork on doors and staircase.

[121] **Balbeuchley House**, *c.*1840, (?)William Scott
Pretty classical country seat on an older site in pinkish ashlar: string-courses, cornice, architraved windows, Ionic-columned porch, shell niches and fanlight. Ornate plasterwork within. Extensive 1802 **steading** was one of the earliest of the new model improved steadings of the district.

Pitpointie Farm, 1883, Edward & Robertson
Opulent mansion built for a Dundee liquor seller, George Willsher, with appropriate decoration everywhere – eaves, bargeboards, hopper heads, finials, granite columns, windows, cast-iron balustrades, and rich plasterwork within. Thatched game store.

Auchterhouse Kirk Session,
having saved thriftily to install
glass windows in the 17th century,
experienced a wanton woman falling
asleep in the kirkyard during
communion who, resting her head
against the new glazing, went right
through it.

*17th-century plasterwork in
Auchterhouse drawing room*

122 Auchterhouse, principally *c*.1630
Do not be deceived by the unspectacular
appearance of this great house, with its
18th/19th-century roof and loss of skyline. The
interior reveals it to have been a place of
magnificence. Indications of its former quality
from the outside are the string-course, the
corbels for a timber gallery facing the
courtyard, and the elaborately carved dormer
heads found lying in the policies (presumably
removed when the current 19th-century roof
was installed to emasculate its skyline).

Perhaps the first instance in Scotland of
reception rooms being on the ground floor, as an
extension to an older tower. The entrance hall
and drawing room contain enriched ceiling
plasterwork as good as can be found anywhere
in Scotland, compartmentalised and punctuated
by large baluster-like pendants. The drawing
room chimneypiece is sumptuous. The arms
indicate the work of the 7th Earl of Buchan,
and there are plaster effigies of his mother and
sister. Further 17th-century ceilings upstairs,
the plasterwork perhaps by Alexander White.
The policies contain much of interest – not least

Auchterhouse from the south-west

the vaulted ground floor of the **Wallace Tower** lying to the south-east (indicating that what survives has been grafted upon the north wing of a courtyard palace); 19th-century **game store**, **walled garden**, contemporary lectern **doocot**, white 19th-century **laundry** (fittings intact), **lodge**, **brew house** converted to squash courts, and a 17th-century *card table* **sundial** (other 17th-century sundials in the manse – tall and slender – and on the kirk itself). Now a select hotel.

Auchterhouse Village is an unpretentious uplands community. **Whitetops**, *c.*1967, by Baxter Clark & Paul (James Paul) must have startled at first – a fruit salad of large monopitched roofs, splayed rough cast walls and spacious interior (formerly with internal water garden). (Former) **Manse**, 1789, redolent of an increasingly prosperous parish replaced a single-storey 1726 predecessor. Generally like an Improvement farm house, it has deep eaves and a triangular fanlight. Single-storey 1784 rectangular **steading**.

Old Parish Kirk, from medieval Rectangular kirk with 17th-century two-storey entrance tower against west end. Substantial rebuilding in 1630 and 1775 leaves only the outsize Gothic chancel arch entombed within the very flat Presbyterian interior. Medieval octagonal font and 1797 clock. Burial vault to east.

Kinpurnie Castle, 1911, Thoms & Wilkie Opulent white-harled château in 17th-century Scots for Sir Charles Cayzer, entered through the gable between squat turreted drum towers. Generally pretty faithful in style, its squat appearance is entirely the consequence of

Kinpurnie Castle: Below *Entrance façade*. Bottom *Garden front*. Bottom right *Original drawing*

lacking the 17th-century ground floor of
kitchens and cellars. Had what we see been
thus elevated, it would have been truly
majestic. Castellated outlook tower on
Kinpurnie Hill.

Bannatyne House, 17th century
Home of George Bannatyne, the collector of
Scots poetry, the house was Victorianised by
Leslie Ower, but, with its angle turret and
white harling, conveys gentle whispers of its
earlier incarnation.

Hatton Castle, 1575
Large Z-plan château, the main entrance and
staircase of which is in the west wing leading
up to a spacious first-floor hall. The laird's
tower is at the other end, identified by the small
private circular staircase. Restored by Douglas
Forrest – although with a skyline only as
exuberant as the surviving evidence allowed.

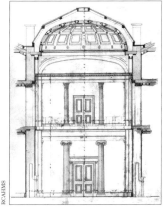

Camperdown House: Top *Section
through the saloon*. Above *Garden
façade*

OUTER WEST DUNDEE
23 **Camperdown House**, 1824, William Burn
This stately home in its magnificent 395-acre
park, one of Dundee's glories, is at the very
highest rank of Scottish country houses. Erected
by the son of the victor of Camperdown, Admiral
Duncan, Viscount Camperdown, it is William
Burn's finest design for a neoclassical mansion.
Entered through a giant, deeply three-
dimensional portico, which occupies the entire
eastern (gable) façade, its principal face to the
south is a masterpiece of understatement: long,
plainly modelled, pilastered, the centre of which
is a two-dimensional rendering of a Greek
monument. It thus enjoys unobstructed views

Camperdown House

over garden and firth. The plan also allowed an uninterrupted sequence of state rooms lining the front; as well as contriving to permit Lady Camperdown to be able to move through her house without meeting either servants or guests if so required. The glory of the interior is a double-height hall, roofed and lit by a stained glass dome surmounted on semi-elliptical pendentives. Now in use as a conference centre. The public **Country Park** includes 18-hole championship golf course, pitch and putt course, horse-riding, tennis, adventure playground and boating pond. (colour page 127)

Right *Ranger Centre, Templeton Woods*. Below *Duncan Mausoleum & Lundie Kirk*

In **Templeton Woods** is a smart angular **Ranger Centre**, 1983, Jack Fulton: jewel-like clarity of triangular form, a shrine of gleaming brickwork and dark timber.

[124]**Lundie Parish Church**,
remodelled 1846 and 1892
Now a Victorian church within a medieval frame, Lundie's appearance is that of T S Robertson – his porch, boarded walls and ceiling. Norman window and remains of a sacrament house in the north wall. Of the memorials, the square-domed **Duncan Mausoleum**, built by Robert Mylne in 1789 against the east gable, is most distinctive. Since it was on the site of the kirk's old chancel, it is appropriate that it should now be used as a vestry.

[125]**Van Leer Tay**, 1949,
Wylie Shanks & Underwood
Like the 1946 Camperdown building (see p.163) – dignity in its simple well-detailed proportion, brick, thin concrete frames and glass.

RIAS Collection

26 **House of Gray**, 1716,
Alexander McGill and John Strachan
Built by the 12th Lord Gray (probably when
Fowlis was abandoned), Gray is an excellent
example of Scottish architecture in transition,
and may be compared to Sir William Bruce's
House of Nairne or the original Mount Stuart,
Bute (see *Ayrshire & Arran* in this series).
Principal pedimented rectangular block is
flanked by ogee-capped stair-towers. Quaint in
ruin, the strength of the original design is
being rediscovered in its current restoration
(after years of partial restoration and
abandonment) and limewashing by Simpson &
Brown. Painstaking jigsaw activity is piecing
together the interior of tall, light apartments,
smokey-blue panelled doors, timber cornices,
and gilt.

LIFF
Rural hillside hamlet with a wonderful view
over the firth, haunted by wood pigeons and
the scent of wild garlic, that has lured so many
Dundonian exiles. The **Parish Kirk**, 1839, by
William Mackenzie, sits businesslike in
mercantile Gothic in its well-groomed kirkyard.
A Gothic **hearse house**. The imposing **Watt
Webster Monument**, 1809, David Neave,
records the Watts of Logie and the Webster of
Balruddery with style – classical columns and
fine incised detail (but lacking urn).

(Former) **Manse**, 1763
Harled, ashlar dressings, pedimented gable,
oculus, finials, etc, in Scots 18th-century
classical completed for the Revd James
Playfair. His son James became Scotland's
most austere neoclassical architect (notably
Cairness House – see *Banff & Buchan* in this
series); James' son, William, architect of
Edinburgh, became Scotland's greatest
exponent of neoclassical architecture.

Above *House of Gray from* Vitruvius
Scoticus. Below *Liff Parish Kirk*

The powerful House of Gray,
whose original seat Fowlis was,
built both Broughty Castle and
Castle Huntly, and, indirectly
Invergowrie House. The Grays
always moved on, from Fowlis to
House of Gray and, in the 19th
century, from House of Gray to
Kinfauns Castle. The most famous
member was the Master of Gray,
banished by James VI for the crime
of procuring the death of Mary
Queen of Scots in England whilst
employed to intercede on her behalf
(an accusation subsequently shown
to be largely erroneous).

McKean

St Marnoch's: Below *Rood screen.*
Bottom *Sacrament house.* Bottom
right *As drawn for the* Building
Chronicle *in 1855*

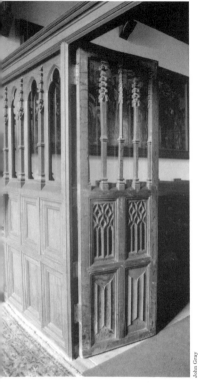

Royal Dundee (Liff) Hospital, 1874,
Edward & Robertson
Huge, symmetrical baronial psychiatric
hospital with spiky skyline. Art installations,
including a mural by Alberto Morrocco, form
part of an art therapy initiative.

St Marnoch's Parish Church, Fowlis Easter,
from 1453 (colour page 128)
Scotland's finest surviving small medieval
parish church: long, rectangular and aisleless.
Well built but plain exterior, save for the
elaborate southern door with its ogival hood-
mould, and the 15th-century window in the
west gable. The interior of Lord Gray's
Collegiate Kirk (raised to that status in 1538)
is its glory: medieval wall paintings, rood
screen, doors, font, sacrament house and alms
dish. The 1480 painted panels depict biblical

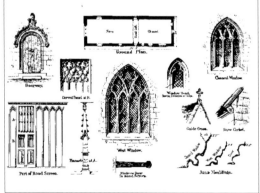

170

characters in Scots costume. Elegiac kirkyard with tombstones, medieval cross and hearse house, 1841. The castle can be seen across the den of the Fowlis Burn in which basks the (disused) 18th-century mill.

Fowlis Castle, 1640
Relic of a much larger courtyard palace, seat of the Lords Gray. This surviving, picturesque block with its great chimney and turreted stair-tower, largely featureless, was almost certainly a residential wing within a larger courtyard which extended horizontally in each direction. Pleasing ivy. Yellow brick dormer-heads much, much later. The **Schoolmaster's House**, 1855, has a satisfying symmetry with its projecting central bay. The **Walkmill Bridge** is 18th century. The corrugated iron **Village Hall**, 1925, has been created from two First World War army huts.

The Knapp
Delightfully rustic bosky glen of the Knapp Burn, adorned with cottages, 18th-century mill (colour page 128), mill house, much belonging to the Rossie estate. Some cottages, i.e. **Parkview Terrace** and the **Old Schoolhouse**, 1872, built with shuttered concrete lined as ashlar, were reputedly servants' cottages for the Rossie dowerhouse (the Knapp – demolished). **Doocot Cottage**, early 18th century, is unreasonably picturesque: its crow-stepped lectern doocot converted to a cottage with fanlit door: the north wall rising above the ridge with three crow-stepped gables capped by ball finials.

Benvie
Ancient site signalled by superb 9th-century incised cross slab – cross on one side, fierce warriors on the other; related in style to the

Below *Fowlis Castle as drawn by Timothy Pont, c.1592*. Middle *Fowlis Castle as it is*. Bottom *The Knapp*

slab formerly at Invergowrie. Only fragments of the large kirk indicated by Pont remain. The early 19th-century **mill**, on the Fowlis Burn, is largely intact. **Benvie farmhouse**, 18th century, belies itself: this elegant white structure is an early 20th-century rebuilding after fire. **Grayburn**, Benvie Road, 1905, was designed by Patrick Thoms for his uncle. Possibly the purest Arts & Crafts cottage in Scotland, it nestles below swooping slate roofs, low slung eaves and behind long rubble walls.

Grayburn (colour page 128)

RIAS Collection

INVERGOWRIE

Odd village mercifully bypassed. That perceived from the main road is but the tip of the iceberg. The rest straggles in copious quantities down to the shore, the station and the original church. It figures in *Wynton's Oryginal Chronikall*. The rectangular shell of **St Peter's** (or Dargie – Pont delineates the long peninsula of Dergow, although naming the building as Kirk of Innergowrie), possibly 16th century, now beached on its mound down by the shore. So also (before they were buried in land reclamation betwixt rail and road) used to be two ancient stones called the Goors of Gowrie, of which Thomas the Rhymer uttered:

When the Goors of Gowrie come to land
The Day of Judgment is at hand.

Tombstone, burial enclosure, medieval and later details. The village became a company village with the success of the Bullionfield Paper Mill whose castellated relic squats by the burn to the north. **Swallow Hotel**, 1870, Campbell Douglas, a substantial, rubbly baronial house and testimony to the ambitions of Bullionfield's owner, is diminished by its extension.

Invergowrie House

The bump at the bottom of Invergowrie Park has variously been attributed to a medieval motte, and to the location of a telescope belonging to an 18th-century salt who liked to keep an eye on the Firth (or maybe radicals approaching from Dundee). It is an ice-house.

127 Invergowrie House, *c.*1600

What can be seen today was extended in 1600, greatly reconditioned and altered by William Burn in 1837. Patrick Gray added a smart new wing, new stair-tower, and dormer windows carrying his initials and those of Anne Napier his wife. The result was a stylish 17th-century U-plan house (like Careston) with corner stair-towers. The quality is indicated by the stair corbelled from the first floor. Stonework would originally have been harled.

128 Prospect Business Centre, Technology Park, 1864, Charles Kinnear

Spiky château rescued from abandonment as mansion to serve as high-tech service centre. Originally the Gows, it has the Frenchified roofscape, High Victorian gables, and barge-boards of the period. It sits, as a benevolent grandparent, to its sprawling, brightly clad metallic space-children in their beautifully landscaped playground. For that is the Dundee Technology Park: a transformation, if ever there was one, of the belief that work in Dundee necessitated dark Satanic mills. Of this bright new world, the brightest is the **Grianan Building**, 1987, Nicoll Russell Studio. It is a factory with a difference: upon three sides, a glazed pavilion perched on cream-coloured columns, the upper storey (a good pun on the word) a clerestory, whereas the ground floor is opaque. Idiosyncratic gutter details. The fourth corner has been cut away in response to the brief to relate to old Scottish cottages: rubbly stone with references to crow-steps and Frank Lloyd Wright. The General Accident **Data Processing Centre**, 1990, Parr Partnership, is a two-storey, shining white, grey-roofed quadrangular pavilion, entered through its corner into a double-height hall. The offices have to have opening windows. (colour page 128)

Top *Prospect Business Centre*. Above *Grianan Building (colour page 128)*

Late Victorian Invergowrie

Invergowrie Parish Church, 1909,
John Robertson
Built with money from Lady Armitstead as a
riposte to Lady Kinnaird's patronage of All Souls
Episcopal along the road, this decoration-free
chunky Gothic displays the stonemason's craft to
good effect. The late 18th-century **toll house** is
pleasant, single-storey and harled with a
prominent projecting bow. The 1849 **manse**,
likewise harled with stone margins, has a
pedimented entrance. **Bullionfield Recreation
Club** (former Free church, 1844), rectangular box
with Romanesque tower was enlarged, 1906, by
Thoms & Wilkie. The aggressive **All Souls
Episcopal**, something very confident in bullish
red stone, 1891, by Hippolyte Blanc, contains a
stone pulpit, marble reredos and excellent fittings.

Station Crescent, Invergowrie, from 1912,
William Gauldie
The feuing for Easter Mylnefield was drawn up
in 1882, but it is Gauldie's hand that is
dominant. **7–13** are two pairs of semi-detached
Arts & Crafts cottages. In 1924, Gauldie
returned across the road, harled, red-roofed
and idiosyncratic. **1–5 Station Terrace** are
red brick villas with decorative brackets and
tile hanging by J Hutton who also designed
Brantwood (No 13) for himself, but drowned
before he occupied it.

Tayside, Kingoodie

KINGOODIE
Mining and quarrying village, the hard stone
from its quarries ideal for sea wall and harbour
work. Although the quarries were no longer
worked after 1895, **Linlithgow Place**, 1920s,
is an excellent pair of Scots stone and slate
cottages for quarry workers, well detailed by
Patrick Thoms. **Tayside** is a 1952 conversion

of several quarrymen's cottages into a smart split-level river house by Sinclair Gauldie.

LONGFORGAN

Beautiful bypassed village consisting of a single street of whitewashed single-storey 18th-century and later cottages with appropriate honeysuckle and clambering foliage spattered with later Victorian and inter-war additions, mainly between 1885–1914, when Dundonians came to rusticate.

Above Longforgan Mercat Cross surmounted by a lion. *Left* Parish Kirk

Parish Kirk, 1794

Elegant rubble box kirk rebuilt upon 15th-century original (when 18th-century agricultural prosperity required space for a larger congregation) enhanced by the retention of the picturesque 1690 tower symmetrically placed against the west gable, a tiny stone spire protruding through the tower's balustrade. The interior was bombed out, 1900, by Alexander Hutcheson, in the interests of the ecclesiological refurnishing. Screens by Sir Robert Lorimer, 15th century, and 1698 memorial slabs and good 16th-19th-century tombstones. The ground floor of the entrance tower was once the village gaol.

The **School House**, 1833, John Bell, has stone Tudor Gothic details and porch. The **Elms**, Main Street, 1910, Thoms & Wilkie, is recognisable by its stone, eaves, tiny central window and dormers. Thoms & Wilkie were responsible for other Main Street houses – the row of three Arts & Crafts cottages – **Westerlea**, **St Colme's** and **Glomach** – and the 1912 villas **Ashlea** and **Maywood**. **Modwenna** (former manse), 1823, David Neave, is a large two-storey building with three central bays projecting to the south in a shallow bow; good interior details.

In 1684 Earl Patrick recorded how he found Huntly Castle upon inheritance, and what he did with it. *My grandfather made this purchase from the Lord Gray at which time save that the land was speciall good it was a place of no consideratione, fit for nothing else but a place of refuge in time of trouble wherein a man might make himself a prisoner ... I wish that everie man that has such houses would reform them; for who can delighte to live in a house as in a prisone ... My father ... put on an inteer new roofe upon the Castle and Jamm which before had ane old scurvie battlement ... The house stands upon a verie stubborne rock ... The house itself was extremely cold: no access there was to the upper part of the house without going through the hall even upon the most undecent occasions of drudgery*

Right *Castle Lyon (or Huntly) in the late 17th century with its new parterres, bowling green, topiary etc.* Below *Castle Huntly in 1798 drawn by Robert Scott.* Bottom *Castle gates*

The Croft, 1895, J Murray Robertson Substantial home of considerable charm grafted upon an earlier farm. A busily picturesque design of bays, corners, neuks, plaster panels, large chimneys, diamond-paned glass, and receding roofs to each storey: inflated cottage style. The late 17th-century **Mercat Cross** is a Corinthian column surmounted by a lion (for Patrick Lyon, Earl of Strathmore) upon a square pedestal and octagonal base.

Castle Huntly, from 1452
Built by the Barons Gray, Huntly clasps a crag that surges out of what was once the floodplain of the Tay (now, in no small measure to Huntly's 18th-century proprietor George Paterson, that floodplain has become the rich fields and orchards of the Carse of Gowrie). Originally a tall L-plan tower house with vaulted lower storeys, Huntly was extensively altered after purchase by the Lyon family in 1647.

Patrick, 1st Earl of Strathmore's account of the castle and its alteration is preserved at Glamis. He renamed the building Castle Lyon, and transformed its medievalism into a country seat, adding Renaissance gardens, terraces, statues, avenues, doocots, ice-house, etc, most of which survive. Extended again in the 18th and 19th centuries, Huntly has been expropriated by the Scottish Home & Health Department as a young offenders' institution which appears to generate the same *esprit de corps* in its inmates as that allegedly apparent in public schools. The 17th-century **North Gate** is outstanding, relocated 1783: square gate piers with attached classical columns are topped with stone spires like those at Moray House (see *Edinburgh* in this series), flanked by graceful curvilinear walls.

Exceptional help in the production of this volume has been received from Colin Wishart, to whom most of the visual impact of the volume will be due; pursued closely, with our thanks, by John Gray of the District Council Planning Department, Stanley P Turner, formerly of the University of Dundee, the photographic collections of the University Library, Dundee District Public Libraries, and the National Monuments Record of Scotland. We are particularly indebted to Clara Young, Keeper of Art, the McManus Galleries; Anna Robertson, Assistant Keeper of Art; Malcolm Thomson, Studio-M; to Paul Smith, Dundee District Council, and to Sinclair Gauldie for their architectural drawings; and to Dr James McIntosh Patrick and Dr Jacob for permission to reproduce beautiful paintings. The Planning Department has been particularly helpful, particularly the assiduous researches of Adam Swan and Neil Grieve (now at Duncan of Jordanstone). We are also indebted to Michael Shafe, Deputy Librarian at the University, Alan Wightman, Iain Rennie, Page & Park, the Parr Partnership, Bobby Black, Andrew Nicoll, Carl Fisher Sibbald, the Chief Architects' Department, Dundee District Council, Stewart Tod & Partners, Messrs T Lindsay Gray, Dick Peddie & McKay, Craig Downie of Studiodownie, and Tayside Regional Council Architects. As usual, the genial staff of the Royal Commission on the Ancient & Historical Monuments of Scotland have been most forbearing. Particular thanks are due to Sinclair Gauldie, PPRIAS, Enid Gauldie, the late Thomas Thoms, PPRIAS, and Professor Alan Lendrum, all of whom were kind enough to contribute knowledge and advice to the original edition. Advice was also received from Angus MacDonald, Arthur Wright, PPRIAS, Michael Merchant, Ian Gow, Catherine Cruft, Roland Paxton, Anne Riches, Richard Emerson, Ian Flett, Robert Dron, Jeff Lonsdale, John Yellowlees, Geoffrey Stell, the late John Clark, Dr Robin Evetts, Dick Dewar, and the late David Wishart. Paul Clark's thesis on Thoms & Wilkie was of particular interest. Staff of the Dundee District Libraries, particularly Mr Kett, were most helpful as was the Buildings Office of the University of Dundee and JJ Herd of the North British Traction Group. Invaluable assistance in production was given by Helen Leng, Wendy Gardiner, Dorothy Smith, our families and other animals.

References

Jute and Flax Mills in Dundee, Mark Watson (Tayport, 1990); **The Life & Times of Dundee**, Whatley, Swinfen & Smith (Edinburgh, 1993); **One Artful & Ambitious Individual**, Enid Gauldie (Dundee, 1989); **The Dundee Book**, Billy Kaye (Edinburgh, 1990); **Dundee on Record**, RCAHMS (Edinburgh, 1992); **Medieval Dundee**, Elizabeth Torrie (Dundee, 1990); **Glimpses of Old & New Dundee**, A H Millar (Dundee, 1925); **Haunted Dundee**, A H Millar (1923); **Dundee in 1793 & 1833**, Annette Smith (1991); **Old Dundee**, Andrew Cronshaw (Edinburgh, 1988); the excellent handbooks by the Abertay Historical Society - particularly **Architecture & Architects in Dundee**, **Mains Castle & the Grahams of Fintry**, **Broughty Castle**. **Dundee Textile Industry 1790-1885** (the papers of Peter Carmichael) edited by Enid Gauldie was of particular help, as were the handbooks of the British Association's visits to Dundee in 1912-68; the publications by Messrs William Kidd in the late 19th century; **Dundee Celebrities** by William Norrie; **The Scottish Building Chronicle**; **The Builder**; **The Ecclesiologist**, the **Baronial & Ecclesiastical Antiquities of Scotland** by Robert Billings; **Theatrum Scotica** by Captain John Slezer; the **History of Dundee** edited by James Maclaren; and the **Castellated & Domestic Architecture of Scotland** by David MacGibbon & Thomas Ross. Thanks are due to the Libraries of the Royal Incorporation of Architects in Scotland and the Edinburgh Architectural Association for permission to reproduce from and to consult their volumes; and to the National Library of Scotland for permission to reproduce from the maps of Timothy Pont.

INDEX

A

Adam, William 14
Affleck Castle 157
Affleck's Lodging 13
Aitken, G S 58, 86, 129, 141, 142, 143, 148
Albany Rd 141-2
Albany Terrace 118
Albert Institute 43-4
Albert Square 46-7, *52*, 53
Albert St 135
Alexander, John 65
Alexander St 123
Alexander, William 40, 44, 55, 116, 118, 131
Allan & Friskin 164
Alloway Terrace 158
Ancrum Rd 103
Anderson, A B 115
Anderson, Sir R Rowand 145-6
Anderson, W J 23
Angus, George 20, 48, 53, 55, 117
Annfield House 87-8
Arbroath Rd 136
Ardshiel 92-3
Armitstead, George 90
Armour, Cornelius 31
Arnhall Drive 93
Arnhall Gardens 93
Arrol, Sir William 82
Arthurstone Library 131
Arthurstone Terrace 131, 135
Arup, Ove 29
Auchinleck Castle 157
Auchterhouse 165-6
Village 166

B

Balbeuchley House 164
Baldovan 162-4
House 161
Baldovie 154
Balfour, Sir James 8
Balgay House 95
Balgay Rd 102
Balgray Building 163-4
Ballumbie Castle 154
Ballumbie House 154
Balmossie 153
Balnacraig 141-2
Bank St 22
Bannatyne House 167
Barlow, Crawford 82
Barlow, W H 82
Barnhill 151
Barrack Rd 116
Barrack St 57-8
Museum 56-7
Baxter Clark & Paul 35, 47, 80, 84, 151, 159, 166
Baxter, D W 148
Baxter, David 56, 112, 132, 134, 162
Baxter family 33, 34, 43, 76, 90, 135
Baxter, George 134
Baxter Pk 135-6
Baxter Pk Terrace 135
Beard, Bennett & Wilkins 163
Beecham, Sir Thomas 18
Bell & Farquharson 88
Bell, John 175
Bell, Samuel 10, 15, 23, 60, 66, 67, 75, 85, 115, 152
Bell St 48
Benvie 171-2

Bett Brothers 122
Bingham Terrace 136
Binrock 90
Birrell, G 122
Bissett, Christopher 32
Black, James 55, 117, 145, 152, 161
Blackness 98, 105
Blackness Avenue 88
Blackness House 95
Blackness Library 89
Blackness Rd 95-6, 102
Blackscroft 32
Blaikie Johnston Withers 75
Blanc, H J 142, 148, 174
Bodley, G F 122
Boece, Hector 11, 20
Bonar Hall 69
Botanic Gardens *72*, 94
Bouch, Sir Thomas 82
Bowbridge Works 131
Braddock, Thomas 119
Brewster, J 56
Broughty Castle 7, 145-6
Broughty Ferry 144-51
Beach Crescent 147
Brook St 146
Camphill Rd 149-51
Castle Green 146
Douglas Terrace 147
Fisher Town 146
Fort St 148
Gray St 148
Hill St 149, 150
King St 146-7
Orchar Gallery (former) 147-8
Public Library 148
Queen St 148
Shore 147
Broughty Ferry Rd 137
Brown, James McLellan 17, 129, 133, 149, 157
Brown St 99
Browne, Sir George Washington 18
Bruce, John 43, 122
Bruce, John & Son 86
Bruce, Son & Morton 143
Brunton, R 122
Brunton Voigt 164
Bryce, David 45, 46
Burke, Ian 20
Burke (Ian) Martin & Ptnrs 122
Burn, William 20, 22, 61, 64, 88, 155, 164, 167, 173
Burnaby Street 94
Burnet, Sir John 16
Butterfield, William 100

C

Caird Hall 17-18, *50*
Caird, James 16, 17-18
Caird Park 160-1
Caldrum Works 122-3
Camperdown Docks 29-30, 127, 167-8
Camperdown Works *107*, 109-11
Cappon, T M 36, 77, 131
Carbet Castle 125, 150-1
Careless, William 32
Carmichael, Duncan 151
Carmichael, Peter 33, 34
Carnegie, Andrew 56
Carolina House 138

Castle 6, 11
Castle Hill 19-20
Castle Hill House 20
Castle Huntly 176
Castle St 10, 11, 16, 23-4
Chalmers, William 138
Chapelshade 114-19
Churches:
All Souls Invergowrie 174
Auchterhouse Old 166
City Churches 59-61
Congregational, Broughty Ferry 146
East, Broughty Ferry 148-9
English Chapel 10
Gilfillan Memorial 63-4
Glasite Chapel 37
High Church, Kinghorn Rd 119
Invergowrie 174
Liff 169
Lochee West Kirk 112
Longforgan 175
Lundie 168
McCheyne Memorial 88
Meadowside St Paul 65-6
Methodist, Ward Rd 55-6
Murroes 156
Ogilvie 132
Old Mains 161
Panmure Trinity 45
Queen St, Broughty Ferry 148
Ryehill 86
South, Monifieth 152
St Aiden, Broughty Ferry 145, 146
St Andrew's Cathedral 66-7, *70*
St Andrew (Trades) 10, 14, 37-8, *51*
St Clement 11
St Francis Friary 103
St James, Broughty Ferry 148
St John's Cross 88
St Joseph 102
St Luke, Baldovan 162
St Luke, Broughty Ferry 125, 148
St Margaret, Barnhill 151
St Mark (former) 85-6
St Marnoch, Fowlis Easter 128, 170
St Mary 61, *69*
St Mary, Broughty Ferry 148
St Mary, Forebank 121
St Mary, Lochee 111-12
St Mary Magdalen Episcopal 116-17
St Mary Magdalene, Blinshall St 100-1
St Mary's in the Fields 11
St Ninian, Lochee *107*, 111
St Ninian, Longtown Rd 158
St Patrick 131
St Paul's Episcopal Cathedral 19, *49*
St Peter 86-7
St Peter, Invergowrie 172
SS Peter & Paul 124
St Rule, Monifieth 152
St Salvador *106*, 122
St Stephen, Broughty Ferry 146
St Vincent RC 158

Steeple Church 60-1
Stobswell 132
Strathmartine 162
Trinity (former) 130
Ward Rd Congregational 56
Whitfield RC 158
Wishart Memorial (former) 36
Churchill, Sir Winston 22
City Chambers 16
City Square 16-19, 41
Civic Graveyard 13
CJFP Architects 86
Claverhouse *126*
Bleachfield 161
Claypotts 139-40
Cleghorn St 103
Clepington Rd 129
Clepington School 124
Clock Tower warehouse 30
Clunas, David 123
Cockburn, Henry 67, 145
Coe & Goodwin 100, 116
Coffin Mill 101
Coia, Jack 124
Coldside Library 129
College of Commerce 102
College of Technology 48
Commercial St 39, 42-4, *52*
Comprehensive Design 40
Conlon, A R 103
Constable, Vernon 142
Constitution Terrace 117
Corbie Hill 11
Courier Building 44-5
Court St *106*, 123
Cousin, David 40
Couttie's Wynd 62
Covell Matthews 99
Cowgate 35-6
Cox Brothers 47, 98, 109
Cox, G A 111
Cox, George 110
Craigie Drive 140
Craigie St 133
Craigiebank 136, 138
Craigiebarn *108*, 140
Craigiebarn Rd 140
Crichton St 10, 11, 17, 22-3
Cullinan, Edward 163
Cunningham, David 30
Customs House 29

D

Dalgliesh, Sir William Ogilvy 53
Dalkeith Rd 136
Davidson St 143
DDC Architects 17, 27, 44, 58, 75, 82, 88, 115, 122, 129, 133, 137, 149, 158, 161
Defoe, Daniel 25
Dens Burn 10
Dens Mills 33-4
Dens Rd 131-2
Discovery Quay 26-7
Discovery 26, *51*
Dock St 28
Docks 29-30
Douglas, Campbell 172
Douglas Terrace 118
Draffen & Jarvie 62
Dronley House 164
Dudhope 114-19
Castle 13, *106*, 115-16
Court *106*
House 117-18

Dudhope St 116, 118
Dudhope Terrace 117
Dunbar Park *126*, 158-9
Duncan, George 83
Duncan of Jordanstone
College *71*, 80
Duncarse 90
Dundee 49, *105*
history 6-11
journalism 44
jute 11, 25, 44
Plan 10-11
Public Arts Programme
41, 65, *105*
textile industry 11, 25
Water War 39
whaling fleet 26
Dundee Rd 143
Duntrune House 155

E
Earl Grey Dock 16, 17, 25, 26
East, Harry 132
Eastern Necropolis 136
Edinburgh Artists'
Collective 87
Edward & Robertson 35,
132, 143, 148, 164, 170
Edward, Andrew 156
Edward, Charles 22, 55, 56
Edward I, King 6
Edward, Revd Robert 7, 9,
10-11, 24, 156
Edward Street Mill 101
Eliza St 124
Elliott, Randolph & Co 35
Ellis & Wilson 102
Ellislea Rd 142
Emberton, Joseph 65
Euclid Crescent 48-53, 54
Euclid St 54
Exchange Coffee House 24
Exchange St 24

F
Fairfield Rd 142
Fairley, J G 54, 130, 131
Fairlie, Reginald 103, 124
Fairweather, John 65
Farington St 92
Findlater, J R 91
Findlay & Smith 123
Findlay, J 77, 154
Findlay Stewart & Robbie 58
Fisher (Carl) Sibbald 41
Florence Booth House 113
Foggie, J 136
Forebank 120
Foresters Halls 56
Forfar Rd 134
Forrest, Douglas 167
Fowlis Castle 171
Fowlis Easter 170
Fréchou, Charles 150
Freeman & Ogilvy 139,
140, 162
Friarfield House 58
Friskin, W W 93-4, 102,
103, 112, 124, 158
Fulton, Jack 94, 168

G
Gagie House 156-7
Gardyne Rd 140
Gardyne's House 20
Garland Place 116
Gate Fellowship 85-6

Gauldie & Hardie 40
Gauldie Hardie Wright &
Needham 45, 78, 93
Gauldie, Sinclair 175
Gauldie, W 95, 174
Gauldie Wright & Ptnrs 29, 158
Geddes, Sir Patrick 76, 78
General Post Office 56
Gibbs, James 38
Gibson, Robert 48, 141
Gilfillan, Revd George 63
Gillespie Kidd & Coia 77
Gillespies 39
Girls' High School 54
Glamis Rd 96
Glas, Revd John 37
Gowans, James 109
Grant, Capt J G 145
Gray family 169
Gray, John 41, 65
Gray, T Lindsay 45
Grayburn *128*
Gray's Close 20
Green, W Curtis 162
Greenmarket 27
Green's Playhouse 65
Greyfriars 13
Greywalls 90-1
Grimond family 35, 131, 150
Grove Rd 142
Guardian Royal Exchange
45-6, *52*

H
Hansom, J A 111
Happyhillock Rd 158
Harbour 11, 24, 25-8, *50*
Harbour Chambers 29
Harbour Workshops 30
Harefield Rd 113
Harris Academy 53, 91
Annexe 102
Harris, Bailie William 53
Harris, Revd G A 134
Hatton Castle 167
Hawkhill School 87
Hazel Avenue 93
Hean Brothers 86
Heiton, Andrew 142, 148, 150
Henderson's Wynd 98, 99-100
Henry's Calendar 130
High School 48-54
Annexe 45
High St 12, 13-16, 18-19, 20, *49*
Highbroom 155
Hilltown 119-29
Hilltown West 122
Hobart & Heron 41
Hodge, Albert 45, 89
Holmes Ptnrship 27
Holt & Glover 142
Hood, Thomas 61
House of Gray 169
Howff *52*, 57-8
Hunter, Robert 27
Hutcheson, Alexander 175
Hutcheson, Fisher &
Campbell 159
Hutton & Tough 134, 136
Hutton, J 63, 174

I
Inner Ring Rd 27, 35
Inniscarra 92
Institute for the Blind 84
Invergowrie *72*, 172-4
Grianan Building *128*, 173

House 173
Prospect Business
Centre 173
Ireland & Maclaren 40, 55,
86, 119, 121

J
Jack, W Murray 36
Johnston & Baxter 31, 32, 138
Johnston, Alexander 43, 46, 84
Johnston, J & F 40

K
Keith, Robert 63
Keith, W B D 142
Kelso St 95
Kempsell, Jake 41
Keyhole, The 58
Kidd, William 63
King St 10, 35, 36-8
Kinghorn Rd 119, 122
Kingoodie 174-5
King's Cross Hospital 129
King's Theatre (former) 38-9
Kinnear, Charles 173
Kinpurnie Castle 166-7
Knapp *128*, 171

L
Ladywell 38
Laird, Michael, Ptnrship 26
Lamond, W G 37, 47, 48,
102, 121, 124, 131, 134,
149
Langlands, J H 48, 54, 87,
102, 103, 124, 132, 134,
149
Laurelbank 117
Law, James 146
Lawside Works 129
Lazarim 142
Leslie, David 160
Leslie, J & A 129
Leslie, James 25, 29, 30, 155
Lessels, John 42
Liff 169-70
Lindsay, Joseph 99
Linlathen East Bridge 153-4
Lochee 109-14
Burns Club 109
High St 112
Library & Public Baths
112
Lochee Rd 99
Logie Avenue 102
Logie Estate 17, 102
Logie Works 101
Longforgan 175
Longtown Rd 158
Lorimer, Hew 103
Lorimer, Sir Robert 148,
154-5, 175
Lowe & Barrie 93
Lower Dens 33-4
Loyal Order of Ancient
Shepherds 31-2
Lutyens, Robert 41

M
McColl Scotland 38
McCulloch & Jamieson 135
McFall, Elizabeth 40, 66
MacGibbon, David 145
McGill, Alexander 169
McGillivray, George *49*, *125*
McGonagall, William 82
McIntosh Patrick, J *70*,

127, *128*
Mackenzie, David 24, 44,
55, 114, 118, 136, 152
Mackenzie, W M 83, 84
Mackenzie, William 169
Mackie Ramsay & Taylor 79
Mackison, William 16, 27,
42, 43, 63, 80
Maclaren & Aitken 43, 58
Maclaren, C G 142
Maclaren, David 28
Maclaren, James 21, 29,
47, 54, 58, 61, 64, 85,
88, 90, 111, 112, 113,
117, 139, 141, 142, 146,
147, 148, 150, 151, 152
McLaren Murdoch &
Hamilton 40
Maclaren, Soutar &
Salmond 151
McManus Galleries 43-4, 52
MacPherson, Archibald 119
McWilliam, Colin 122
Madeira St 134
Magdalen Green 69, 82, 83
Magdalen Yard 81-4
Magdalen Yard Rd 83-4
Magnum House 31
Mains Castle 126, 160-1
Mains of Gray 127
Manhattan Works 123
Marine Parade 30
Marryat, Mrs 18
Martin, Hugh & Ptnrs 20,
40, 164
Masson, Kenneth 136
Matthew (Robert) Johnson-
Marshall & Ptnrs 77, 96
Mathewson, George 66, 83,
121, 143, 147
Matthew Building 80
Mawson, Sir Douglas 26
Maxwelltown 122
Meadow Entry 40
Meadowplace Buildings 47
Meadowside 44-5, 47, 56
Meldrum, Andrew Mackie 68
Menart, C J 67
Menzieshill 97
Mercantile Bar 52
Mercat Cross 62
Mercer Blaikie 151
Mid Craigie 157-8
Millar, A H 16
Mills & Shepherd 90, 94,
143, 155
Miln, James 66
Milnbank Rd 101
Miln's Building 64
Monifieth 151-3
Grange House 152
Hill St 152
Queen St 152
Victoria St 152
Monikie 157
Monk, General 8, 13, 14
Montrose, Marquess of 8
Morer, Thomas 13
Morgan Academy 107, 133-4
Annexe 124
Morgan Place 133
Morgan Tower 68-73
Morrocco, Alberto 170
Morrow, Tony 40
Morton's Bond 28
Murraygate 38, 39-42
Murroes House 155-6

INDEX

Mylne, John 62
Mylne, Robert 168
Mystery House 96

N

Neave, David 37, 64, 73-4, 75,
  76, 83, 84, 111, 144, 169, 175
Nethergate 10, 59-62, 65-6, 75
Nethergate Centre 65
Nethergate House 67
Nicoll Russell Studio 55,
  66, 71, 74, 80, 86, 142,
  146, 151, 173
Ninewells Hospital 72, 96-7
Niven & Wigglesworth 44
Norrie, William 39
North Bond 31
North Lindsay St 11, 58-9
Northern College 140
Northwood 108, 141
Norwood Crescent 92

O

Ogilvy, G F M 162
Ogilvy, Sir Herbert 162
Old Bank Bar 22
Old Dundee 6-24
Old Steeple 60, 61
Olympia Leisure Centre 27
Orchar, J Guthrie 148
O'Reardon, John 41
Oswald, J 82
Overgate Centre 20, 62
Ower, C & L 22, 47, 89,
  112, 136, 137
Ower, Charles 144
Ower, Charles (Snr) 29-30
Ower, Leslie 132

P

Page & Park 87
Panmure St 45-6
Panmure Terrace 117, 118
Parish Council Chambers 55
Park Avenue 132
Parkview School 95
Parr, James 143
Parr, James & Ptnrs 23,
  27, 38, 79, 102, 147, 158
Parr Ptnrship 73, 146, 173
Patrick, William 122
Paul, James 166
Paxton, Sir Joseph 135
Peddie & Kinnear 108, 133
Peddie, J Dick 79
Peddie St 88
Pelly, Frances 41
Pennant, Thomas 37
Pennycook Court 71, 87
Perth Rd 80, 81, 85-6, 88-95
Phillips, Alan 98
Phillips, C G L 105
Pierson, Provost 13
Pilkington & Bell 85-6, 88-
  95, 120
Pilkington, Frederick 118
Pillars 14, 18, 50
Pitfour St 103
Pitkerro 154-5
Pitpointie Farm 164
Playfair, James 169
Playfair, Revd James 169
Playfair, William 169
Pont, Timothy 155, 172
Powrie Place 121-2
Princes St 33-5, 41, 132
Property Centre 64

Prospect Place 117
Pugin & Pugin 102

Q

Queen's Hotel 68

R

Rait, David 40
Ralston Rd 141
Reform St 10, 11, 20-2, 50
Regional Music Centre 55
Reid & Greig 65
Rep Theatre 74-5
Rickards, E A 57
Riddoch, Provost Alexander
  10, 22, 25, 40, 67
Ritchie Dagen & Allan 64
Robbie & Wellwood 158
Robert the Bruce 6
Robertson & Orchar 84,
  123, 129, 130, 131, 148
Robertson, J M 28, 46, 48,
  77, 92, 95, 112, 139,
  141, 142, 150, 152, 176
Robertson, John 174
Robertson, T S 55, 146, 150
Robertson, W W 56
Rockwell Central School 124
Roodyards Burial Ground 137
Roseangle 81-2
Ross, Donald 91, 141
Ross, Thomas 61, 145
Rowand Anderson & Paul 78
Rowantree Cres 158
Royal Dundee (Liff)
  Hospital 170
Royal Exchange 46
Royal Infirmary 116
Royal Tay Yacht Club 125, 143
Royal Victoria Hospital 95
Rustic Place 116
Ryehill Lane 87

S

Sailors' Home 28
St Helen's 91-2
St Joseph's Convent 119
St Roque's Library 32-3
St Salvador's St 122-3
Salvation Army Hostel 55
Sandeman St 124
Scott, Sir George Gilbert
  19, 43-4, 60, 61, 148
Scott of the Antarctic 26
Scott, William 22, 55, 136,
  156, 164
Scouring Burn 10
Seabraes Gentlemen's
  Lavatory 80
Seafield Works 70, 84
Seagate 11, 30-3
Seagate Gallery &
  Printmakers' Workshop 32
Seymour Lodge 89
Shambles 11
Sheriff Court 55
Shore 27, 28-9
Shore St 24
Sibbald, James 42
Sibbald, R & J 82
Sibbald, Sir Robert 10
Simpson & Brown 20, 64,
  122, 169
Simpson, Archibald 53
Simpson, Robert 131
Slessor, Mary 36
Slezer, Captain John 10

Small, Robert 6, 7, 8
Small's Wynd 77
Smirke, Sir Robert 162
Smith, George 24, 53
Smith, W J 27
Smoor, France 156
Snell, Brian 65
Snowden, R 122
Somerville Place 117
Soutar, C G 102, 140, 143
Soutar, Charles 144
South Balluderon 164
South Mills 99
South Rd 112
South Tay St 73-4
Southey, Robert 25
Spence, William 19
Springfield 86
SS Peter & Paul RC School 124
Stark, Malcolm 63
Steell, Sir John 136
Stephen, J F 90, 110, 123
Stewart, Sir John 23, 24
Stokes, G H 136
Strachan, John 139, 169
Strathern Rd 141
Strathmartine Castle 162
Strathmartine Lodging 9, 13
Strathmartine Rd 129
Sunningdale 108
Sutherland, Scott 62, 159

T

Tay Bridge 82
Tay Park 92
Tay Square 74
Tay St 10, 69
Tay Works 99, 105
Taybank Works 136
Taylor, John 29
Tayside House 27-8
Tayside Region Architects 134
Tealing House 164
Technology Park 128, 173
Telford, Thomas 25, 28, 30
Templetown Woods 168
Theatre Royal 23
Thistle Hall 64
Thoms & Wilkie 62, 91, 92,
  93, 94, 113, 139, 140, 141,
  151, 153, 166, 174, 175
Thoms, Patrick 90, 172, 174-5
Thomson Brothers 123
Thomson, Frank 23, 38,
  88, 89, 129, 138
Thomson, H & F 146
Thomson, Harry 58
Thomson, James 16, 26,
  32, 56, 96, 102, 131
Thomson, James & Harry 138
Timex 163
Tod, Stewart 100
Tough, James 118
Town Hospital 9
Town House 9, 14-15, 16
Trades Hall 10, 15
Trinity Church Hall 132
Trottick Mains 161
Tullidelph Rd 103

U

Umpherston & Kerr 34, 101
Unicorn frigate 30, 51
Union Hall 15-16
Union St 10, 64
University 76-80
  Arts Tower & Library 77

Belmont Hall 78-9
Bonar Hall 77
Carnegie Physics
  Building 78
Geddes Quadrangle 71, 78
Medical Sciences
  Institute 79
Old Medical School 77
Old Technical Institute 77-8
Scrymgeour Building 77
Students' Association
  71, 79
Upper Dens 34-5, 51

V

Van Leer Tay 163, 168
Vault 11
Verdant Works 99-100, 105
Victoria Dock 30
Victoria Rd 120, 129-31, 144
Vine 69, 83-4

W

Wallace Craigie Works 136
Wallace, James 80
Wallace, William 6
Wallace Works 131
War memorial 119
Ward Rd 55-6
Waterhouse, Alfred & Son 47
Waterhouse, Paul 47
Waterworks 134
Watson & Salmond 94
Watson St Housing 137
Watson's Bond 31
Wedderburn family 7
Wellgate Centre 38
Wellwood Leslie 80
West Bell St 55
West Ferry 108, 137, 138-
  40
West Park 90
West Port 98
Wester Powrie 159-60
Western approach 81
Western Cemetery 91
Westfield Avenue 86
Westgrove Avenue 92
Westpark Centre 90
White, Alexander 165-6
Whitehall Crescent 62-4
Whitehall St 62-3
Whitfield 158-9
  Skarne estate 158-9
Williamson, William 92
Willison St 58
Wilson, Charles 65, 90, 91-
  2, 117
Wilson, David 40, 62, 65
Wilson, Hugh 65
Windmill Bar, Hilltown
  122
Windsor Place 85
Windsor St 85
Wishart Arch 36
Wishart Centre 36-7
Wishart, Colin 75, 122
Wishart, George 7, 36
Womersley, Lewis 65
Wood, Lizanne 41
Wylie Shanks &
  Underwood 168

Y

Yeaman Shore 27
Young & Meldrum 66, 68,
  118

PICTORIAL GLOSSARY

1. Ashlar (dressed stonework in smooth blocks).
2. Balustrade (line of small columns usually along a balcony or parapet—in this case in ironwork).
3. Bow (projecting semi-circular bay).
4. Buttress (Stone column supporting the walls, usually of a church).
5. Cherry-cocking (small stones set between larger blocks of stone).
6. Corbel (stone supporting a projection above, one end embedded into a wall).
7. Cornice (projecting top of a wall).
8. Crowstepped gable (a gable in the form of a series of steps).
9. Curvilinear gable (wavy-shaped gable).
10. Cupola (roof light).
11. Dormer window (window projecting through the roof plane).
12. Drum tower (circular one-bay tower, usually for staircase).
13. Eaves (overhanging edge of roof).
14. Fanlight (patterned glazed window above a door).
15. Finial (crowning feature e.g. of tower).
16. Keystone (centre stone of an arch).
17. Palazzo (a building in imitation of an Italian Renaissance palace).
18. Pavilion roof (piended, or hipped—sloping on all four sides).
19. Pediment (triangular feature).
20. Pilaster (flattened column attached to a wall).
21. Quoin (long and short protuberant stones emphasising the corner).
22. Stringcourse (stone course or moulding projecting from the surface of the wall).
23. Tracery (window pattern, usually in churches).
24. Venetian window (three-part window, the centrepiece raised and curved).
25. Wallhead or nepus gable (gable rising through the roof in the front of a building).

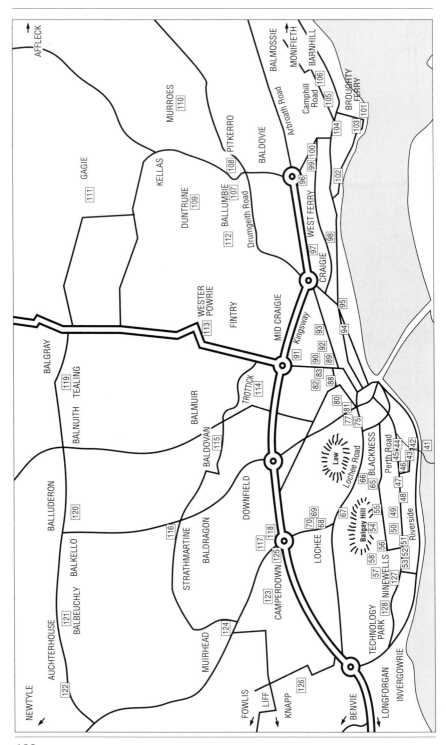

AFFLECK

NEWTYLE

MURROES
110

GAGIE
111

KELLAS

PITKERRO
108

DUNTRUNE
109

BALLUMBIE
107

Drumgeith Road
112

BALDOVIE

BALMOSSIE

MONIFIETH

BARNHILL

Arbroath Road

Camphill Road
106

105

BROUGHTY FERRY
101

104

103

99 100

96

WEST FERRY

102

CRAIGIE
97

98

95

WESTER POWRIE
113

FINTRY

MID CRAIGIE

Kingsway
93

91

90

92

89

82 83

88

80

94

TROTTICK
114

BALGRAY

TEALING
119

BALNUITH

BALMUIR

BALDOVAN
115

81

77

75

BALLUDERON

BALKELLO
120

STRATHMARTINE
116

DOWNFIELD

BALDRAGON

Law

Lochee Road

BLACKNESS

Perth Road

66

65

45 44

42

46

43

41

47

AUCHTERHOUSE

BALBEUCHLY
121

MUIRHEAD
124

CAMPERDOWN
125

117

118

123

LOCHEE

70

68

69

67

Balgay Hill

54

55

48

49

50

Riverside

51

52

53

42

56

58

57

NINEWELLS
127

128

TECHNOLOGY PARK

FOWLIS

LIFF

KNAPP
126

BENVIE

LONGFORGAN

INVERGOWRIE

183

ARCHITECTURAL GUIDES TO SCOTLAND

A MAD IDEA: the belief that by the millennium the whole of Scotland can be compressed within 28 vivid, pocket-sized volumes, painting the history and character of each place through the medium of its surviving or demolished architecture.

"Good armchair reading with their exotic mixture of fact, anecdote and personal comment"
- Colin McWilliam, The Scotsman

SERIES EDITOR: Charles McKean

— Currently available —

EDINBURGH by Charles McKean 1982 & 1992
DUNDEE by Charles McKean and David Walker 1985 & 1993
STIRLING AND THE TROSSACHS by Charles McKean – *reprinting 1994*
ABERDEEN by W A Brogden 1986
THE SOUTH CLYDE ESTUARY by Frank Arneil Walker 1986
CLACKMANNAN AND THE OCHILS by Adam Swan 1987
THE DISTRICT OF MORAY by Charles McKean 1987
CENTRAL GLASGOW by Charles McKean, David Walker and Frank Arneil Walker 1993
BANFF & BUCHAN by Charles McKean 1990
SHETLAND by Mike Finnie 1990
THE KINGDOM OF FIFE by Glen Pride 1990
ORKNEY by Leslie Burgher 1991
ROSS & CROMARTY by Elizabeth Beaton 1992
THE MONKLANDS by Allan Peden 1992
THE NORTH CLYDE ESTUARY by Frank Arneil Walker and Fiona Sinclair 1992
AYRSHIRE & ARRAN by Rob Close 1992
BORDERS & BERWICK by Charles A Strang 1994

— Forthcoming —

GORDON by Ian Shepherd 1994
CENTRAL LOWLANDS by Richard Jaques and Allan Peden
SUTHERLAND & CAITHNESS by Elizabeth Beaton
DUMFRIES & GALLOWAY by John Hume and Judith Anderson

ARE YOU BUILDING UP THE SET?

The RIAS/Landmark Trust series is winner of the *Glenfiddich Living Scotland Award 1985*
These and other RIAS books and books on World Architecture are all available from RIAS
Bookshops at 15 Rutland Square, Edinburgh EHl 2BE, Tel 031-229 7545
and 545 Sauchiehall Street, Glasgow G3 7PQ, Tel 041-221 6496